"If you are strugg[...]
this book offers re[...]
empathy, humor, [...] honesty. You'll find a friend
within these pages."

Sheila Walsh, cohost of *Life Today* and author of *It's Okay Not to Be Okay* and *Holding On When You Want to Let Go*

"Where is God in the midst of your pain? What happens when you're too tired and exhausted to pray? Whatever you're going through (the death of a loved one, an illness, a divorce, etc.), it's comforting to know that you're not alone. Niki Hardy has been through the valley of the shadow of death and eloquently unfolds her powerful story with raw, vulnerable honesty that cuts to the heart of the human condition. I would recommend this book to anyone going through a health crisis and to anyone struggling with the issue of real, active faith in the midst of a silent, raging tempest."

JD Chandler, national media personality, K-LOVE Radio Network

"Filled with life-giving hope, practical help, and the perfect blend of real-life humor we need when life falls apart! This book holds the truth we need and the companionship of the friend we want to walk through days that leave us gasping for air and seasons that make us wonder how we'll ever survive. Through the death of loved ones, her own battle with cancer, and one hard thing after another, Niki asked God tough questions and fought to find the answers we all need. I highly recommend *Break Free from Survival Mode*! I'm getting a copy to keep and a few to give away, and you should too!"

Renee Swope, bestselling author of *A Confident Heart* and former radio cohost, Proverbs 31 Ministries

"Niki Hardy is the voice you need to hear when life goes the opposite of what you imagined. I'm buying *Break Free from Survival Mode* in bulk to stock our arsenal of books that we keep around to give away to friends and family. This book is a gift."

Myquillyn Smith, *Wall Street Journal* bestselling author of *Cozy Minimalist Home*

"This is a gem of a book—just as its author is a gem of a person. Niki is vulnerable and real about pain and suffering, whether her own or others', but she doesn't leave us there. She points us back to God and gives us spiritual encouragement and some down-to-earth practices that we can engage in if we want to thrive and not just survive the tough times. A must-read for anyone who feels they are in a pit of any kind right now—or anyone who ever has been or will be, which just about covers us all, I think."

John Peters, rector of St. Mary's, Bryanston Square, London, England

"My friend Niki knows firsthand what it's like to feel like everything is falling apart, and somehow, in the midst of it all, draw closer to God. Niki leads us on a journey that will take each one of us straight to the feet of Jesus. And she does it with stunning vulnerability, biblical truth, and even humor. (Reading along, I couldn't help but laugh as I imagined her, with her British accent, talking about her 'bum,' 'the loo,' and 'rubbish.') I would recommend this beautiful book to anyone who doesn't simply want to survive but to rise up and thrive."

Jennifer Dukes Lee, author of *It's All Under Control* and *The Happiness Dare*

Break Free
from
Survival Mode

Break Free
from
Survival Mode

7 WAYS TO **THRIVE** THROUGH HARD TIMES

Niki Hardy

© 2019 by Niki Hardy

Published by Revell
a division of Baker Publishing Group
PO Box 6287, Grand Rapids, MI 49516-6287
www.revellbooks.com

Spire edition published 2022
ISBN 978-0-8007-4116-7
eISBN 978-1-4934-3589-0

Previously published in 2019 under the title *Breathe Again*

Printed in the United States of America

The author is represented by MacGregor & Luedeke Literary

Baker Publishing Group publications use paper produced from sustainable forestry practices and post-consumer waste whenever possible.

22   23   24   25   26   27   28   7   6   5   4   3   2   1

To Mum and Jo

You led the way.
You showed me how.
I miss you.
Every day.

To Al

My best friend, my hubby, my partner in crime, my HB.
No matter what life chucks our way,
you're the man I want to live it with.
Thank you for believing in me.
I love you.

To my beans—James, Sophie, and Emma

Remember these three things, always:
God loves you desperately.
So do I.
And wherever life takes you,
the flapjack tin will always be waiting, full.
I love you . . . more.

Even though I walk through the valley of the
   shadow of death,
 I will fear no evil,
for you are with me;
  your rod and your staff,
  they comfort me.

Psalm 23:4 ESV

Contents

Contents

I'm Sorry You're Here . . .
No Wait, I Take That Back

In this world you will have trouble.

John 16:33

I have come that they may have life, and have it to the full.

John 10:10

I'd been home less than twenty-four hours when I got the call from my sister, Claire. It was time. I'd hardly been back home in Oxford, England, long enough to throw anything in the wash or put my suitcase back in the attic, but it was time. Time to head back to Vancouver, Canada, to my mum's house, where she'd lived since marrying my stepfather nearly twenty years earlier. She'd been battling aggressive small-cell lung cancer for the last year, and I'd just spent two precious weeks visiting her. How could it be time? Had things deteriorated that fast?

I chucked some mismatched clothes and my wash bag back into my suitcase, landed a firm but quick oh-my-goodness-I've-got-to-go peck on Al's cheek followed by one for each of the kids, and then dashed back to the majestic coast of the Pacific Northwest.

Mum was barely conscious by the time I arrived at the hospital, yet she appeared to have been waiting for me, the last of her kids, to arrive. Turning her head as I perched on the edge of the bed, she smiled weakly, the corners of her mouth curling slightly upward, relief filling her eyes.

"You made it," she mumbled.

As her breathing became labored and she slipped unconscious, we held her hands and prayed. She passed away as we—my sisters Claire and Jo, and our stepfather with his grown children—looked on helplessly.

"In this world you will have trouble . . ."

Six short years later, Claire had to make another call. It was time. Again.

With an ominous sense of déjà vu, I went through the motions as if acting in a play I'd rehearsed only once before. Once again it seemed like just a few hours that I'd been home. By then Al and I had moved with our three small kids to Charlotte, North Carolina, to plant CityChurch, and I'd been back in England for a week visiting my sister Jo in Torquay. It was now Jo's turn to be fighting that same terrifying disease: aggressive small-cell lung cancer. When I'd hugged her goodbye, stroking her soft, fuzzy, chemo-bald head, my bubbly, vivacious chef of a sister may have been a shadow of herself physically, but she'd still been the same old feisty, belligerent girl I knew and loved who could crack a joke like a stand-up comic. How could it be time? Had things deteriorated that quickly?

It was just after Christmas, and we were having a brilliant time sightseeing and freezing our butts off in DC when the international number flashed up on my phone. My stomach lurched. I just knew. I'd thrown my passport into my bag just in case this happened, but it had felt like a betrayal to Jo's strength to fight on, so I'd studiously ignored the fear warning me to pack my little black dress and pumps. All I had with me were jeans, fleece socks, my winter boots, and the rather gaudy fake-fur earmuffs I'd had to buy to save my ears from the biting DC wind. It would have to do.

Once again I kissed Al and the kids goodbye, found a seat on the first flight from DC to London, and crossed the Atlantic deep in fear-motivated prayer.

As the train from London came to a stop, I stepped down into my father's waiting arms. We stood clinging to one another, our hug tight and lingering, oblivious to the other passengers navigating awkwardly around us. His unuttered fear and grief were deafening.

"When I told her you were on your way, she smiled and said, 'Oh, it's that close, is it?'" Holding me at arm's length, he looked me in the eyes. "She knows it's nearly time, and she doesn't seem frightened. That's good. That's a good thing," he reassured us both.

The pain of seeing my father ache for his dying daughter tore me apart. It's just wrong for a parent to lose a child. It just is—it's out of order.

And I like order.

Like our mother before her, Jo's eyes filled with relief as I pushed open the hospital door and sat beside her. With the faintest curl in the corner of her mouth, she smiled our mother's smile.

"You're here," she whispered.

Claire, Dad, and I held her paper-soft hands as her breathing became labored and she slipped unconscious. We prayed, told her we'll always love her, and that she could let go. Tears fell as we said our goodbyes. She was just forty-four years old. It was New Year's Eve 2011, and somehow that was fitting. Jo loved a good party, and maybe, just maybe, she knew each year we'd raise a glass to her and smile, the faintest curl in the corner of our mouths, as the clock strikes midnight.

"In this world you will have trouble . . ."

Just six short weeks later, with my jet lag but not my grief a thing of the past, I sat in a cold, clinical hospital room and was told I too had cancer. Not lung cancer but rectal cancer.

Rectal cancer?

Are you kidding me? That's a double whammy right there. *Rectal* and *cancer* are two words that should never meet let alone hang out together. How would I live that down? More to the point, would I live? Had the heat-seeking missile of death finally locked in on me? Was it now my time?

Would my kids be getting a call like the ones I got from Claire, telling them it was time? Would Al be calling Claire and Dad in some weird twist of fate? Would they be the ones jumping on a flight, dashing to my side, and holding my hand? Would I manage to smile, the corners of my mouth turning up slightly, relief flooding my eyes, knowing the end was close?

Would my breathing become labored as I slipped unconscious while they prayed, held my hands, and told me I could go?

Would I pass away at just forty-three?

"In this world you will have trouble . . ."

I'm Sorry You're Here

I am. In fact, I wish you weren't.

I know, that's weird. What author wishes no one will read her book? That would be bonkers. But it's true. I'm sorry you're here because it probably means your world is painful and difficult right now. And if yours isn't, then it's likely someone else's is, someone you care about. No one picks up a book with the subtitle *How to Live Well When Life Falls Apart* when life's happy and skippy. You'd never read a book about finding more when life hands you less unless life really has handed you way less than you bargained for—so I hate that for you.

My story isn't especially unique, and yet that's exactly why I want to share it with you. Not so you'll feel sorry for me. Lord knows I've done enough of that already. No, I want to sit with you, sharing bits of my story and stories of others who've been where you are, because although the specifics might belong to me, the pain, grief, exhaustion, and the rubbish we tell ourselves belong to us all. Bad news sucks the air right out of our lungs. We hold our breath, hands to our mouth in disbelief as we listen to a life-changing diagnosis, the slam of the door as our husband walks out, or the voice of the banker explaining our house is going into foreclosure. Then, as the aftershocks overwhelm us and we cope as best we can, we struggle to keep breathing, gasping for each new lungful.

Deep down we're all the same. When life's storms threaten to drown us, we just do our best to keep calm, carry on, and breathe. If I've learned one thing along the way, it's that learning to breathe again is a team sport and we all need a little help along the way.

So, I'm Actually Really Glad You're Here

The fact you're reading this tells me you want more, even though you've been handed a bucketful of less. You want to stand up right where you are and inhale deep lungfuls of fresh, life-giving air. You want your shoulders to drop an inch from where you've been wearing them as earrings, to relax little by little, to feel hope bubble up through the cracks of your broken spaces. I'm thrilled you want to lean in and go for it because I truly believe there is more for you.

The second I was diagnosed with cancer I was called a survivor. As you can imagine, I embraced my new title with gusto and wore it with pride. Hardy by name, hardy by nature, that's me. Until after a while I realized that's all I was doing—merely surviving. Then I met others who had shunned the word "survivor" for its more exciting and hope-filled cousin "thriver," and I was intrigued. It sounded so alive and full of hope and energy without glossing over the tough stuff. Thriving sounded like surviving but with life-giving benefits added in free of charge. I wanted that. I wanted what they had. I too wanted to thrive, not just survive.

At the heart of this book is my encouragement that thriving—living the full abundant life God has for us—is possible right in the middle of our heartache, tragedy, and yearning.

Jesus says, "I have come that they may have life, and have it to the full" (John 10:10).

To grab hold of that full life we've got to shatter the myth that seasons come and go, clearly defined by circumstances and emotions. Yes, we experience tough seasons and busy seasons, spiritually dry seasons and seasons bursting with excitement, yet we assume these must be mutually exclusive, separated in time and space, and that it's impossible to experience more than one season at a time. But to live life to the full we must smash this idea that the storms and abundance of life happen in different time zones, separated like quarreling siblings sent to opposite ends of the room.

We endure, we survive, and we forget to look for joy in the midst of deep grief or intimacy in a season of loneliness. And yet, in the unsafe, raw darkness of my grief and cancer, I was surprised to find myself able to hold hands with peace and fear in the same moment. I found I could laugh when all I wanted to do was scream.

We've bought into the myth that a painful season can't be full, that a time of abundance isn't challenging—and this, dear reader, gets my goat. I just don't think it's true, and this is exactly what this book is about: smashing this myth and inhaling all God has for us.

So if you're looking for a book about surviving, this isn't it. It's not about hanging in there, longing for happy, skippy days in the distant future, or plastering on a plastic fantastic smile, pretending life is hunky-dory because you're a good little Christian. As Sheryl Sandberg said, "The question is: When these things happen, what do we do next."[1] This book is about what's next.

I wish we could chat over a cup of tea, but you're there and I'm here, so my words will have to do until I can hug you in person. Either way, let me look you in the eyes and tell you that you matter, you're loved, and you're not on your own in this. I want more for you, my friend, and I'm absolutely confident God does too.

So the practices I share in this book are for you. They help me to take those first life-giving breaths after shocking news or to simply keep breathing when I'm drowning. They help me grasp as much of the full life Jesus has for me as I can lay my grubby paws on. These are my answer to "What next?"

Stuff still knocks the wind out of me on a regular basis. I handle it terribly, throwing ugly, passive-aggressive hissy fits I take out on the dogs. But as I lie awake at night, worrying while the rest of the world sleeps, I come back to these practices and slowly I breathe again, a little more deeply than the day before. And that's my prayer for you too.

I call them "practices" because that's exactly what they are. If you've ever done yoga, you'll know practices are about accepting where we are and refusing to compare ourselves to the human pretzel next to us, all while improving our mental and spiritual well-being. They are about setting our intentions as we inhale deeply before giving thanks and stretching. They are about moving forward into downward dog—despite knowing our life is heading into downward-facing spiral—all while trying not to laugh or break wind, of course.

When I was knee-deep in grief and chemo, I needed someone to show me *how* to grab hold of the life Jesus came to give me, not just to inspire me it was there . . . somewhere. I needed someone to show me *how* to live in the pain, not just get through it. These practices are the way I found to do just that. They are my gift to you.

At the end of each chapter you'll notice two things: a new line in our Thriver Manifesto and some questions. The manifesto is a written declaration of who we are and what we believe as Thrivers, not merely survivors. It will build as you go through the book and learn the practices, dive into the questions, and start to breathe again. I want you to be able to make this manifesto your own, so I made a printable version for you to keep close. You can download it and all the other "gifts" I've created just for you at www.nikihardy .com/breatheagaingifts.

Let's thrive—together!

Before we jump in, it's important we find some solid ground first. When life falls apart and all hell breaks loose, we've no idea which way is up or which way to turn. Afraid and vulnerable, with our world hurtling out of control, we cling to anything that might stop its spinning. The trouble is, not everything that looks stable is solid ground. If we're standing on a quicksand of lies and misunderstanding when the ground quakes, it sends tsunamis of emotions deep into our lives and we fall further apart. The only way to find our firm foundation is to be totally clear about what is truth and what is rubbish, and then throw the trash where it belongs.

Jesus came that we might live life to the full. Let's go grab it.

I am a Thriver.
I believe life doesn't have to be pain-free to be full.

PART 1

Finding Solid
Ground

1

Rubbish We Believe When the Poop Hits the Fan

It's all my fault, God's angry, and now he's vanished

A lie told often enough becomes the truth.

Vladimir Lenin

The thief comes only to steal and kill and destroy.

John 10:10

If God had told me all I needed to do to be healed and cancer-free was stand on one leg in a bowl of oatmeal while singing "God Save the Queen," I'd have jumped right in without taking my socks off. I was desperate for healing.

Who wouldn't be? So when a book about how to receive God's healing anonymously landed on my doorstep, I put the kettle on and dived in. I couldn't wait to hear what this book had to say, as I was confident God could zap my tumor from its dark orifice with the snap of his heavenly fingers. Unfortunately, I never made it past the first few pages and my tea lay forgotten.

I couldn't believe my eyes. The words stung and burned as if I'd sat butt naked on a fire ant nest. This book that promised so much encouraged me to *just* lay hold of my healing, to *just* have enough faith, to *just* believe, and even to *just* lay claim to my God-given, abundant (which implied "fully healed") life. I'm paraphrasing somewhat, but you get the gist of what it said. I couldn't read on.

Rather than feeling encouraged and hopeful—expectant even—that God can and does heal, guilt, fear, and hopelessness welled up alongside frustration and sadness. It was that small four-letter word that did it. By using the word *just* at every turn, the author had a gun loaded with insinuations pointed right at me, holding me hostage.

Each sentence implied it was my fault God hadn't healed me. I obviously didn't have enough faith, I wasn't good enough, or I hadn't figured out what God was teaching me. If my faith was stronger, or if I prayed certain prayers and *just* believed in my *stone-cold, stubborn* heart, God's blessings would pour forth from heaven and I could claim my healing *and skip through life's meadows* fully restored (the italics are my passive-aggressive frustration seeping out). It placed my healing firmly on my own shoulders. If I wasn't healed, it would be my fault.

It was hurtful and damaging, not to mention theological bunkum that reminded me of bogus faith healers in white suits proclaiming the prosperity gospel at the expense of the hurting and hopeless. But annoyingly, it sunk in. Despite knowing it was nonsense, I was left feeling inadequate and somehow to blame for my suffering.

I've never met another woman who doesn't believe some sort of rubbish about herself or who truly believes how wonderful she is, have you? Believing lies about ourselves seems to come free with our extra X chromosome, along with hormonal mood swings and the eternal search for a life-completing shade of lipstick. But when life falls apart and stinks worse than a week-old tuna sandwich, our perspective of what is true about God, our circumstances, and ourselves is rocked. It's hard to know what's true and what's not, and lies love to grow and take root in this fertile soil.

Friends, it's time to call the lies what they are because this rubbish steals our abundant life right out from under our noses and keeps us locked in ever-shifting, life-sucking quicksand where it's impossible to catch our breath. This is why it's so important to deal with the lies before we do anything else. Then and only then can we find solid ground to build on.

Over the years I've believed more than my fair share of these lies, and never more so than during my grief and pain. The more I believed them, the more I watched myself untethering from God as I lost touch with his truth. As she carried her unborn son, who she knew wouldn't survive more than a day after his birth, my friend Maria said that she had to kill her fear before it killed her.[1] In the same way, we must kill the lies we believe before they kill our ability to live life to the full—but we can't do this if we don't know what they are. So the first thing we've got to do is identify them and bring them out of the shadows into the light.

The Lies We Believe

Self-Trash

Lies prefer to stay hidden and undetected, so let me ask you this: Have you ever walked numbly out of a doctor's office and imagined the shock waves of your diagnosis spreading out to affect everything and everyone you love? Or perhaps you've blamed yourself for not getting pregnant or failing to find Mr. Right despite the ticktock of your biological clock. Maybe you've been up night after night believing the fallout from your broken marriage will never end and happiness will always elude you.

These are the kind of things lies whisper into our pain, and I've been there, done that, got the T-shirt, and been to therapy to prove it. Apparently we're not alone.

When psychologist Martin Seligman researched thousands of people who've experienced suffering and how they dealt with it, he discovered three often-held core beliefs that stunt our recovery and therefore magnify our suffering:

Personalization: the belief we are to blame—it's all my fault.

Pervasiveness: the belief all areas of our life will be affected.

Permanence: the belief the aftershocks will last forever—life will always be like this.[2]

As I read these, everything in me shouted, "Yes, yes, YES! Me too! I believe them all!"

They've taken hold in the dark of night. I've cried myself to sleep churning my own personal versions over and over. These lies are so plausible, so real and tangible, I can reach out and touch their cold exterior. I call them my "self-trash."

It's All My Fault

Despite being told I'd done nothing to cause my cancer, I still managed to blame myself. I've always eaten the entire apple—core, pips, stalk, the whole nine yards. Maybe it was that? Perhaps it was because I'm lazy and have never washed my fruit and veg properly, or maybe I ignored the symptoms. Then, to cap it all, I managed to heap on more blame for all the disruption, pain, and worry my illness and treatment rained down on everyone, from my family and friends to the lady who booked my appointments.

I constantly apologized for anything and everything. I still do. When the family's waiting in the car outside yet another ladies' loo at the third petrol station we've had to make an emergency stop at in the last half hour, I apologize repeatedly no matter how many times they tell me it's fine. As another whopping medical bill lands with a thud on our doormat, I hand it to Al apologetically, with a million "I'm so sorry's."

Even though my cancer wasn't my fault—not even the fault of the genes I was born with—I still believed somehow it *was* my fault. If it wasn't the apple pips or the unwashed fruit, then God must be angry with me. Maybe I'd done something to deserve this, or he was testing me. Perhaps my faith wasn't strong enough for him to heal me. Whatever the reason, however illogical, I believed somehow my cancer was my fault.

Every Part of My Life Is Affected

When my bum got cancer, it felt like my whole life got cancer. I hated the way it seeped into every nook and cranny, the small everyday things as well as the big whoppers. I didn't have the energy to even cook for my kids, and I watched as kind friends ferried them to their activities. It was a gift, but it was a visible sign the cancer was seeping out from where it started, weaving its way through my body and life, and I believed it robbed me of my role as mum.

Then there was the impact I saw on the big important parts of life: I assumed that one argument meant our marriage was falling apart and on the fast track to divorce, or that every teenage outburst meant the kids were so worried and messed up they were doing drugs to numb their pain. Even as I began to get better, I couldn't do things like run the trails the same way I used to. Just walking the dogs became a game of connect the dots between the public bathrooms in the park and porta-loos on neighborhood construction sites, all the while praying for the presence of loo paper. My cancer traveled with me. Where I went, it went, and I couldn't see a part of my life where its tendrils weren't wrapped around, choking me.

Life Will Always Be Like This

As the fog of cancer descended, I couldn't see how life could ever return to how it was BC—before cancer. The life I saw stretching ahead seemed permanently stained by my current cancer-colored reality. Surely I'd always feel this way. How could I ever feel normal again? The surgeries had completely replumbed me, and I couldn't trust my digestion for longer than it took to make a cup of tea, so I imagined a life of bathroom-seeking anxiety panning out ahead of me. Not to mention the ever-present reality that the cancer might return. I wanted my life back—all of it—but I couldn't see that ever happening.

And what if I didn't make it? If the kids had to hold my hand as I breathed my last, would they ever recover, or would they be scarred for life? I just couldn't see how life could change.

It was as if a second cancer of lies ate away at me along with the tumor. See for yourself in this list of even more lies I claimed for myself.

I believed no one really understood what I was going through.

I believed people saw me as pitiful, a charity case.

I believed I had to cope with a smile and be strong.

I believed I was different from everyone else.

I believed my ostomy bag and scars made me ugly and unwanted.

I believed I was a burden.

I believed I was broken and unmendable.

I believed I was weak—only weak people get sick.
(I didn't believe this about Mum and Jo, but I sure did when it came to me.)

Then there were the lies I believed about God, which is kind of tricky and awkward given I'm a pastor's wife.

God-Trash

To make myself feel like a normal human being during treatment, I would hide the bulging ostomy bag on my belly under floaty sweaters (or as my kids called them, my "baggy" clothes) and camouflage the bags under my eyes with industrial-strength concealer. And since I never lost my hair during chemo, each Sunday I would sit in church looking just like BC Niki. Except I wasn't.

I love our church, so I never felt the need to fake a smile or hide my cancer, and from the front we were as real and honest as we could be. But since I didn't look sick on the outside, I appeared to have it all together on the inside. No one knew what was really going through my head as I went through the motions on my darkest days. I call these lies my "God-trash."

God's left me.

God's fed up with my moaning, angry outbursts, and neediness.

God doesn't care anymore.

God's busy with more important things (like the Ebola outbreak in Africa) and more spiritual people (like Julie at church, who's annotated her whole Bible—in color!).

God doesn't see me, and if he does he ignores me.

God doesn't love me like everyone else.

God's not as good and merciful as I thought.

I've done something to make God angry.

God's trying to teach me something I'm just too dense and tired to figure out.

I'm the exception when it comes to God's love and grace.

God's mad at me for some mysterious reason.

Maybe you resonate with a few of these immediately and can pinpoint your own daily battles. Or perhaps you're feeling a little smug, grateful your beliefs are so strong you don't struggle with this nonsense. But twenty years in ministry have taught me we all believe this trash at some level—however buried or camouflaged—and never more so than when tragedy strikes and our defenses are down. This is why, if we are to find solid ground and begin to breathe again, we must deal with them.

Dad, Dandelions, and Digging Deep

When I was a kid, my dad showed me how to pull dandelions out of our lawn. He told me there's no point in just snapping off the stalk and spiky leaves; it was important to dig out the entire root if I didn't want them to grow back and stab my bare feet next summer.

Trying to find God's full life in the midst of our less-than life without dealing with Seligman's three P's or our God-trash and self-trash is like dancing through the sprinkler in the heat of summer on a lawn full of spiky dandelions. We can do it, but it's not nearly as much fun, and we'll finally give up and head inside.

When I wrestled my first dandelion from the lawn, I was amazed at how big and strong its single taproot was and how deep it had grown into the soil. Seligman is right: the three P's, along with other lies we believe about God and ourselves, magnify and prolong our suffering. If we want to do more than just build resilience and heal from the painful things in life—if we want to live life fully in the midst of the pain and beyond—we must pull up those lies by their roots. God is calling us to grab hold of his abundance right where we are, but the call of God always requires us to leave something behind. To live abundantly, even in the midst of pain and suffering, we must leave behind the false beliefs holding us back.

So, if you're serious about grabbing the most out of the life you've been dealt, get a pen, a pad of paper or one of those fancy journals you got last Christmas, and your Bible, and find somewhere quiet, because this is where we start to learn to breathe again. If you've got small children, hide in the bathroom, get a neighbor to watch them, or take a long bath. Anything to love yourself enough to dive in.

The questions at the end of each chapter are where the magic happens. They are super important and I'd hate for you to skip them. Because while the practices are the map, it's not until you start walking the roads themselves (by doing the work in the questions) that you make progress to where you want to be.

Jesus came to give you abundant life—now go grab it.

I am a Thriver.

I believe life doesn't have to be pain-free to be full.

I reject the lies of the world about who and whose I am.

LEARNING TO **BREATHE AGAIN**

Take a moment to do this exercise.

First, name something you believe about your season right now, then ask yourself why you believe it. Why does it frighten or worry you? Why do you churn it over in your mind or scream it to God in anger?

Then ask why again, and again.

Maybe add in a "So?" or "So . . ." Here's the idea: you're on a treasure hunt, and the core belief is the gold. The self-trash or God-trash you unknowingly believe is the dandelion root that needs pulling out.

Let me show you what it looked like for me when I did this exercise.

My first belief or cry out to God was, *I can't believe God would let this happen to me and my family.*

So I asked, Why?

Because I've done so much for him, loved him, followed him—heck, even moved across the world for him— done my best at every turn.

Why?

Because I thought he loved me.

Why?

Because that's what the Bible tells me and I've seen his love for other people.

So . . .

He obviously doesn't love me like he loves them.

Why?

Because I'm not good enough.

33

Ouch. There it is. The core belief. *I'm not good enough for God to love me.*

I had to dig deeper to find the lie behind it.

So . . .

God's grace is there for everyone else, but it doesn't apply to me.

So . . .

I'm the exception. I have to earn his love.

Boom. Found it: *I'm the exception and I have to earn God's love.* Do you see how it works?

The root holding on in the soil of my life and faith was the idea that I have to earn God's love. For a pastor's wife who is passionate about grace, this was a doozy.

Despite years of preaching and teaching about God's grace and the freedom of not needing to earn his love or salvation, I still believed, somewhere buried deep inside, that I was the exception and had to measure up to be loved (and therefore healed) by God. In my head I knew it was utter nonsense, but it's no wonder I spiral down and away from him when things get tough. No wonder I couldn't grasp all he had for me.

Now it's your turn, friend. If I can do it, so can you. If we want to kill the cancerous lies before they kill us, we have to flush them out by spraying them with Day-Glo paint to identify them. Only then can we remove them.

As we repeat this exercise over and over, we identify more and more lies. The more lies we see, the more we'll be able to remove, and the more we remove, the softer the lawn come summer and the fuller the life we can live.

So rinse and repeat, my friend. Rinse and repeat!

Dear Lord, you're the God of truth, but I still believe a whole load of rubbish about both of us. I just can't help it, especially when I'm struggling with everything I'm dealing with. I'm sorry for believing this nonsense.

Digging around for the roots of these weeds sounds like no fun at all, but I know I can't live abundantly with them buried deep, affecting every part of my life and faith. Lord, give me the courage to look for them. Shine your light so I can see where they're hidden in the darkness, and give me the strength to pull them out.

You are the way and the truth and the life, so show me your way and free me to receive your truth so I can live life abundantly today.

In your name, the name that never lies. Amen.

2

The Truth We Need
When Our World Is Rocked

Life doesn't have to be pain-free to be full

Indeed, one can be deceived in many ways; one can be deceived in believing what is untrue, but on the other hand one is also deceived in not believing what is true.

Søren Kierkegaard

Then you will know the truth, and the truth will set you free.

John 8:32

I sat in a sun lounger and exhaled, my freshly painted toes peeking out cheekily from behind my beach read. Claire plonked herself wearily beside me and, with a sigh of "we made it, now we can finally relax," grabbed her book.

Getting both families away to celebrate Christmas and New Year's together had been twelve months in the making. We'd saved our pennies, researched resorts, ring-fenced our calendars, and flown hundreds of miles to be together. Finally we were exactly where we wanted to be—side by side on plush, comfy loungers, fruity cocktails in hand, and ready to do nothing except catch up, snooze, wish Jo was there, and decide where to stuff our faces at dinner that night.

Little did we know we weren't the only ones happy to be there. Fighting over the remains of a half-eaten burger abandoned by a woman now attempting to burn off its cholesterol in pool aerobics, a couple of blackbirds squawked noisily before making a beeline for my pink cocktail umbrella. I batted them away angrily, narrowly avoiding language more suitable at a fight night than a family resort.

We watched, horrified as the quiet of the pool turned into a scene from *The Birds*. Joined by a flock of feathered friends, they circled and shamelessly attempted to steal anything that looked remotely edible. If I got up for even a second, twenty birds took up residence on my lounger. It looked like our much-anticipated holiday in the sun was going to be ruined.

Just then, beyond the floatie-wearing toddlers screaming with delight in the shallow end of the pool, I saw a young woman in khaki raise her arm and launch a hawk into the air. It swooped over the pool, between the sunshades, and past the cocktail bar before returning to the raw meat in her gloved hand. Then it was off again and again as we oohed and aahed. I waved for the kids to watch, amazed the hotel offered falconry displays.

When the khaki-clad girl and her bird of prey returned the next day and every day after that, I realized this wasn't a show put on for our entertainment but a necessary hotel service providing peace and protection for their guests. Thanks to the hawk lady constantly launching her powerful feathered weapon against the birds, we had a wonderful holiday.

The Truth We Need

When I think about the lies we just identified at the end of the last chapter—the self-trash and God-trash we believe when life's as much fun as a root canal without anesthetic—and I think about how they steal joy, peace, and life from under our noses, it reminds me of that relentless onslaught of blackbirds trying to steal our food and pooping on our holiday. What we need is our own personal hawk of truth ready to launch into the air to send the lies packing. They are as devious and tenacious as those dastardly birds, and we must go on the offensive and counter with some self-truth and God-truth if we are going to find solid ground and start breathing again.

There are so many truths we could talk about here, I could write an entire book on them. (Oh wait, someone already did—it's called the Bible!) But as we go in search of solid ground, here are some of the most helpful ones for when life's fallen apart.

We must send these truths soaring into your heart to re-place the lies we've just uncovered. If we identify the lie but don't plant truth in its place, other lies quickly sneak in and start growing. Soak in these truths and think about them as you rummage for the missing sock in the laundry, reread them after an exhausting day before you zone out on Netflix, and repeat them with every footfall as you walk the dog.

Breathe them in, feel your shoulders relax, and let them settle over you. God breathed life into us at creation (Gen. 2:7) and his breath gives us life each day (Job 33:4), so let's inhale it deeply.

Let's start with some much-needed self-truth.

You Are Loved

Let's start with the big one. I don't care what you say: You. Are. Loved.

When we found out Jo was dying, my dad wished more than anything he could take it from her—even change places with her—and when she died, his grief was the sorrow of a father unable to save his little girl. As a dad, his love was never in question.

His tears for Jo hadn't stopped falling when I told him it was my turn, and I knew he would change places with me too if he could. I never questioned Dad's love for me even though he's not perfect by any stretch of the imagination (sorry, Dad). So why did I question God's love when he is, in fact, perfect?

I wondered whether God only kinda-sorta loved me, or was only happy to love me when I shared my sandwich with the homeless guy on the corner or when I actually felt warm and held. Maybe his love grows proportionately to the amount of time I spend in church? I just couldn't figure it out.

I didn't *feel* loved by him so assumed I *wasn't* loved by him, but the truth is we are loved whether we feel it or not. We may see the heartache of our right-now lives as evidence of his lack of love, but he loves us here too. We are loved 100 percent, unconditionally, with no strings attached. There are no terms and conditions, no small print, no get-out clause. He loves us.

The beauty of God's adoring love is that it's not dependent on how fabulous or not we are (and I'm sure you're pretty fabulous) or conditional on anything we may or may not have done (good or bad). He loves us purely because of who he is and what he's done.

God *is* love (1 John 4:8). He's not just loving, he is love itself. It's not just something he does, it's who he is. He can't help but love us, his kids, passionately because love is the core of his being and all love comes from him (1 John 4:7). Just as my Goldendoodle, Chester, can't help being a dog (a pretty stupid one, I admit, but a dog he most certainly is), God can't help being love. Chester is a dog and God is love—it's who they are.

As Ann Voskamp says, "If love isn't shaped like a cross, it isn't really love."[1] This is the unending depth of grace. What more evidence do we need? There are no kinda-sortas, maybes, or ifs with God's love. He's all in. When we deny his love, we deny who he is, and when we do that we deny ourselves the extraordinary life he has for us. He loves you because he is love, and unlike my father who couldn't change places with either of his children, God took your place on the cross and died so you—yes, you—can live. Yes, he died for all of humankind—but he would have died for you if it was just you here on earth. The proof of his love for you is the cross.

Repeat after me: "I am loved." Say it loud. Say it in a whisper. Write it in lipstick on your bathroom mirror. "I am loved. I am loved!"

Breathe it in, allowing it to refresh your weary bones and spark hope.

You Are Enough

This truth takes a close second to the truth that you are loved, because no matter what life throws at you or how you respond, you are enough.

My cancer diagnosis felt like a personal failure. Ironically, I'd never seen Mum and Jo as failures for having cancer, but when it was my turn I played by different rules. I was sick, therefore I must have failed in some way, which meant I wasn't enough: not strong enough, lovable enough, good enough, nice enough, spiritual enough, worthy enough, you-name-it-I-wasn't-it enough. Then, when I tried to be enough and fill all the gaps, to do all the things I thought would make me enough, that didn't work out so well either.

We are enough not because we fill our gaps but because God does. I am enough because I am in him and he is in me (John 14:20), and he is enough. I hadn't failed, I hadn't let anyone down, I hadn't lacked the magic key to living my fabulous happily ever after. His love for me was and is unconditional, and that makes me enough. The same is true for you too.

Whether we're weak or strong, cry mascara-streaked tears in traffic, admit we're worried we can't pay the next mortgage bill, or are about to walk down the aisle with the wrong guy, we are enough because of *whose* we are, not *who* we are.

Breathe this beautiful truth in, repeating after me: "I am enough because Jesus is enough. I am enough because of whose I am, not who I am."

You Are Seen

Jo lived on the outskirts of Torquay, a seaside town in Devon, England. Her flat sat in a corner of a gray stone

Victorian mansion on a hill that eventually wound down to the sea. A couple of months before she died, I spent time visiting her, enjoying short trips nosing around the seaside shops together and long talks about everything and nothing.

My visit was precious, hard, and over far too quickly. Every day I would run alone along the winding footpaths hugging the jagged clifftops near the flat and feel small and unseen. My sister was in pain and dying, and I was utterly helpless. My God wasn't fixing it, and as the wind whipped my ponytail and my legs burned from the climb, I thought about Jo, Mum, and my family on the other side of the ocean. I felt untethered and powerless, as if living in a parallel universe.

A few short months later Jo died, and my own diagnosis snapped at my heels like a snarling pit bull. That sense of smallness and of being unseen and untethered returned. I didn't like it.

In John 4, when the woman at the well saw Jesus sitting there, she probably assumed he wouldn't notice her and thought she was all but invisible to him. After all, he was a Jew, she was a Samaritan, and Jews avoided and ignored Samaritans. Yet he saw her. Not just how she came to the well alone, bucket in hand, but he saw her pain and loss. He knew her.

Even when we expect to be unseen, we are seen. Even when we feel unseen, God sees us. High above the jagged rocks and crashing waves, God saw me, and even with no one around to hear my expletive-filled cries and prayers, I wasn't invisible. Being alone and feeling unseen can't make me invisible any more than singing along to *Mamma Mia!* and feeling like a movie star makes me Meryl Streep.

We are seen and loved just as we are, valuable just as we are, and matter to God right where we are. Breathe this in and let the truth you're not unseen or ignored tether you to the One who sees you. Say it with me, and say it loud: "I. Am. Seen."

And now let's focus on God-truth.

God's Not Angry

As I lay on my side grimacing, watching grainy images of the inside of my rear end on the screen next to me as my surgeon delicately maneuvered what can only be described as a baseball bat with a camera on its end to get a glimpse of my lymph nodes, I wondered what I'd done to deserve this. Was the universe playing some kind of sick joke on me? Was God too angry to stop it? Surely he must be mad at me for something, I just couldn't for the life of me figure out what it was.

Enduring my internal ultrasound wasn't the first or last time I'd jumped to this conclusion, and I've discovered when the poop hits the fan and lands on my desk, my instinct is to assume God threw it in anger. Maybe you've done the same?

My house is in foreclosure . . . what did I do to deserve this?

My husband had an affair for three years without my even suspecting . . . is God punishing me for having sex before I was married?

This is my third miscarriage this year . . . is God angry I married a non-Christian?

43

The cancer's spread to my lymph nodes . . . what did I
    do to make God so angry?

God's wrath is something I try not to think about too
much—it seems so out of character, too ungentlemanly for
the God of love and mercy, and yet I quickly assume he's mad
at me as soon as the going gets tough.

The problem is, I'm attributing his wrath to the wrong
situations. Yes, God gets angry, but only at my sin—the stuff I
do that separates me from him. I have to remember that in the
same way he is fully love, he is also fully just, and Jesus satis-
fied this just wrath on the cross because of his love for me.

Assuming our shattered world is the fallout from God's
wagging finger, we beat ourselves with a stick of our own
making. Yes, God gets mad—but not at our pain, not at our
struggles and heartache.

The truth is, God isn't mad at you. He's mad *about* you.[2]

What more can he do to show us? As it says in *The Message* translation, "God didn't go to all the trouble of sending
his Son merely to point an accusing finger, telling the world
how bad it was. He came to help, to put the world right again"
(John 3:17). Do you hear his love, not anger? Let's not take
our difficult circumstances as evidence of God's anger; instead, let's look at Jesus's life and death as evidence of his love.

Breathe in the truth and repeat after me: "God's not mad
at me, he's mad *about* me."

He Will Never Leave You

I thought I was showing up for my regularly scheduled
radiation appointment with my usual friendly consultant,

but the doctor who greeted me that morning was different. It didn't take long to discover she had the bedside manner of a menopausal rhino, and after a perfunctory greeting she snapped on her latex gloves and asked me to bend over.

As you can imagine, I've seen more than my fair share of doctors—some warm, kind, and empathetic, others calm, courteous, and matter-of-fact—but she was the first to treat me like a beaten-up old truck with a leaky radiator. I felt violated and fought to hold back the tears as I got dressed and left. Halfway home I couldn't hold it together any longer. Sobbing, I pulled into the local park and found a secluded bench.

My world had already shattered, and now she had stomped on its remains in her ugly size-ten doctor shoes. As my shoulders heaved and a delightful mix of snot and mascara ran off my chin, loneliness wrapped its arms around me.

Even surrounded by people who love us fiercely, we are the only ones who cry our tears, feel our pain, and fear our fears. It can be lonely, and "suffering is unbearable if you aren't certain that God is for you and with you."[3]

Alone on that park bench, I wondered where God was. I felt so alone. Why couldn't I feel him? Wasn't he meant to live inside me (John 14:20)? Didn't he promise to never leave me (Deut. 31:6)? The gap between what the Bible tells me and what I felt in my bones sucked the breath out of me.

The truth is, God hadn't left me. He was sitting right there on that park bench with his arm around me, valiantly wiping the mascara from my cheeks. He wasn't angry, and he wasn't ignoring me. His heart ached for mine; he was present and listening. How do I know? Because eventually, as I leaned into his promises and away from my feelings, the chasm between the two narrowed and I began to breathe again.

When Jesus tells his disciples he has to go away but will send the Holy Spirit, he tells them eleven—yes, eleven—times he will be with them even after his death (John 14). He wants us to know it too, and let's not beat ourselves up if it takes more than eleven times to sink in.

As we walk out of the doctor's office stunned by a diagnosis, wrap our arms around an epileptic toddler, hold yet another negative pregnancy test, or wonder how we're going to get through the week, he is with us and whispers, "Be sure of this—that I am with you always, even to the end of the world" (Matt. 28:20 TLB). When we turn our blotchy, ugly-crying faces toward him, we discover he's right there; he never left us after all.

Breathe it in and repeat after me: "He will never leave me."

He Has Good Stuff for You Here

"'For I know the plans I have for you,' declares the LORD, 'plans to prosper you and not to harm you, plans to give you hope and a future'" (Jer. 29:11). Have you ever had someone throw this verse at you in an attempt to brighten the cold, dark reality of your sucky world? It can feel like confetti at a funeral.

As the nurses hooked up my cocktail of chemo drugs and anti-nausea meds, the last thing I felt like I was doing was prospering. Cancer was ravaging my body, not just harming it, and who knew if I even had a future beyond cancer. It wasn't the most hope-inspiring situation I could have dreamed up. So much for Jeremiah's words.

Soon after I'd finished treatment, Al asked me to preach on "The Plans God Has for Us When Life Is Hard" and gave me this Scripture. As you can imagine, I was less than delighted. But as I dug deeper into the text, I was surprised to discover the Israelites and I actually had a lot in common. Exiled in a foreign land, wondering what had happened to the promises God made to their forefathers, they were having a terrible time. It sounded so terribly familiar, and I resonated with their cries for help.

Rather than explaining how God would rescue them, Jeremiah tells the Israelites that God wants them to marry, have children, grow crops, seek peace with their neighbors, and pray for Babylon (Jer. 29:4–7). In other words, get on, live life, and stop waiting. Dig roots right where you are; be present in your present situation. The plans God has are here and now.

As I look back over my years of grieving and treatment, I see that I found the most of what God had for me when I made the most of where I was, right where I was, without waiting for easier days that may or may not materialize.

God has good things for us even when bad things have happened, and we find them right where we are.

Breathe in the truth and repeat after me: "God has good things for me even here, in the midst of my hardest moments."

Life Doesn't Have to Be Pain-Free to Be Full

This little ditty by Robert Madu stuck in my brain the moment I heard it:

> Facebook, Facebook, tell me how my life should look.
> Instagram, Instagram, tell me who I really am.[4]

Because they do.

Except it's rubbish.

Happy, healthy women showing off happy, healthy families with happy, healthy bank accounts stare back at us as we scroll away in the supermarket checkout lane. It's not surprising we feel lacking as we compare our anything-but-shiny life to their bright-and-smiling, just-for-the-camera lives.

We live in a glossy culture where if it looks glossy it must be glossy. We are bombarded with glossy perfection a thousand times a day on TV, online, and in magazines where beautifully curated homes with pristine children adorned in neutral tones skip playfully through the forest or read quietly in dappled sunlit tree houses.

No one posts pictures with captions like "This is me fighting with my teenager who I found sneaking out last night" or "This is my cute new bag (where I stash my secret little orange bottle of pills)." And I've never seen a selfie with the hashtags #lonely, #depressed, #abused, #unworthy, #ashamed, or #unlovable.

We hope if we present life as perfect, it will *be* perfect. So we fake it, paralyzed by the thought of anyone knowing the truth. The world's image of what abundant life looks and feels like is a myth; it's smoke and mirrors perpetuated by social media, TV, and movies, and it's fueled by our own insecurities. "An abundant life is a perfect life" is a myth. "We can create it ourselves if we work hard enough, are good enough, and please God sufficiently until he blesses us" is a myth. Jesus never said, "I have come that you might have life, and have it more fabulously."

We compare our everyday imperfect reality with other people's moments of curated perfection. We make ourselves both creator and curator of our abundant lives, but we'll never get there, because what we're trying to create is an illusion.

Then, when tragedy or heartache leaves us gasping for air, we feel disqualified from any kind of abundant life—fake or real—so we miss out.

The crazy part is, I did this exact thing as I wrote the first draft of this book. Between you and me, I found this writing thing ridiculously hard, as it's definitely not my zone of genius, and in the "vomit it out and just get words on a page" stage I hated it. I'd read what I wrote and curl into a ball, thinking I was a terrible writer, the book would be rubbish, and no one would read it. Why? Because I was comparing my vomit-stage beginnings to other authors' brilliant, edited, and published finished books. So much so that I had to stop reading anything but beach reads until I finished.

It's easy to do the same in life, especially when life's difficult. We compare the reality of our broken, painful, right-now life with other people's perfectly filtered social media posts and end up feeling like lonely failures. We exclude ourselves from the very thing we long to experience so desperately— the full life God has for us.

I'm not a particularly tidy or organized girl, but the one thing I like to compartmentalize is my life. I allocate things— emotions, circumstances, outfits, workouts, you name it— into specific boxes: good, bad, painful, right, wrong, fun, challenging, and even boring. It feels safe to have everything neatly labeled, but I've realized that life with God isn't so black or white. It's more like an artful mixing of black and white into the most beautiful dove gray.

I've felt deep worry and hope in the same moment, held hands with both peace and panic, and danced with one arm around joy and the other around pain. I've discovered that opposing emotions can somehow nestle side by side in the palm of my hand.

It's blown my mind, to be honest. I don't understand how, but hooked up to IVs and heading off to surgery I've felt comforted and alone all in the same moment. As I waited for pathology results, I trusted God fully and yet doubted him deeply. Don't ask me how it works (perhaps time travel or a split personality?), but what if it's God's abundance fully present even in the middle of a life that's anything but abundant?

Life isn't clear-cut after all, and I've learned this profoundly simple truth: life doesn't have to be pain-free to be full.

I hope after breathing in these truths, your feet have found solid ground, a firm foundation for learning to breathe again. We've identified the lies, uprooted them, and replaced them with truth. As you head into the practices, I want to encourage you to keep meditating on these truths—especially the ones that feel least at home in your heart. The love letter on the next page is a wonderful way to do that.

I am a Thriver.

I believe life doesn't have to be pain-free to be full.

I reject the lies of the world about who and whose I am.

I embrace the truth that I am loved, seen, and enough, and that God loves me, isn't mad, and will never leave.

LEARNING TO **BREATHE AGAIN**

Here's an excerpt of a love letter from God to you, written entirely in Scripture verses. I've no idea who originally collated this, but I've read it over rooms packed with aching hearts and seen the truths it contains heal the most broken and paralyzed places. So now I'm sharing it with you. Breathe it in, letting God's Word do its work.

Highlight the verses that speak to you most; write them on sticky notes and post them on the fridge. Underline verses you struggle with or that grate on you, and ask yourself why that might be. Go back to the exercise in the last chapter to figure out what lie might be behind that discomfort.

If you're more of a listener than a reader, I've made an audio version where I read the entire letter over you to help you relax and let God's words sink in. Hop over to www.nikihardy .com/breatheagaingifts to download it.

A Love Letter from God (Author Unknown)

My dear sweet child,

I am not distant and angry, but am the complete expression of love (1 John 4:16). And it is my desire to lavish my love on you simply because you are my child and I am your Father (1 John 3:1). I offer you more than your earthly father ever could (Matt. 7:11).

Every good gift that you receive comes from my hand (James 1:17), for I am your provider and I meet all your needs (Matt. 6:31–33). My plan for your future has always been filled with hope (Jer. 29:11) because I love you with an everlasting love (Jer. 31:3).

My thoughts toward you are countless as the sand on the seashore (Ps. 139:17–18) and I rejoice over you with singing (Zeph. 3:17). I will never stop doing good to you (Jer. 32:40), and I want to show you great and marvelous things (Jer. 33:3).

If you seek me with all your heart, you will find me (Deut. 4:29). Delight in me and I will give you the desires of your heart (Ps. 37:4). I am able to do more for you than you could possibly imagine (Eph. 3:20), for I am your greatest encourager (2 Thess. 2:16–17).

I am also the Father who comforts you in all your troubles (2 Cor. 1:3–4). When you are brokenhearted, I am close to you (Ps. 34:18). As a shepherd carries a lamb, I have carried you close to my heart (Isa. 40:11). One day I will wipe away every tear from your eyes and will take away all the pain you have suffered on this earth (Rev. 21:3–4).

I am your Father, and I love you even as I love my Son, Jesus (John 17:23).

God

Lord, I've believed so much rubbish in my life. I need your truth to drown out the lies.

Thank you for these unfailing truths and your love for me that drives them. I find them hard to hear, I find them hard to believe, and yet I want so desperately for *them to fuel the way I live my days. Give me the courage to believe them and the strength to walk in them, especially when things are tough.*

In the name of the One in whom I am enough.
Amen.

3

Practice Makes Better,
Not Perfect

You are braver than you believe, stronger than you seem,
and smarter than you think.

Christopher Robin

For the Spirit God gave us does not make us timid, but
gives us power, love and self-discipline.

2 Timothy 1:7

For years doctors dismissed her symptoms as stress re-
lated, but Leta was convinced her "ulcer" wasn't just an
ulcer but cancer, and hearing about my diagnosis motivated
her to push for an answer. Tragically, she was right.

Leta lived just a year and a half after her diagnosis, but in those eighteen short months she was the poster girl for Thrivers everywhere. With three boys she loved fiercely and a husband trying to deal with his new role as caregiver, she chose to grab life and squeeze every last drop out of it. Even when the cancer spread and the end was in sight, she refused to roll over and give up, choosing to wrestle more life, laughter, love, and connection out of those months than many of us do in a lifetime.

As we sat on her back porch, her new pixie cut more red carpet than chemo ward, she turned to me with a mix of resignation and determination.

"This might be crappy, but it's not going to beat me." She exhaled wearily before breaking into a smile as she pushed herself up to wrap her fourth grader in a bear hug as he walked in from school.

Despite the endless treatments, surgeries, and side effects that often left her too weak to get out of bed, she continued to fight. Yes, fight the cancer, but ultimately fight to find true life in what life she had left.

Did she have endless optimism and gumption the rest of us lack? Nope.

Did she have moments when all she wanted was her old life back? Heck yes.

Did she feel the despair of knowing she'd never see her boys as men? All too well.

Did she ever want to give up? I'm sure.

Did that stop her? Not on your life.

Was she any different from you and me? Absolutely not. She was a southern woman with a gift for home decorating and loving well, but she would be the first to tell you she was no superhero—just an ordinary woman who chose to carve an extraordinary life and legacy from the prognosis that had shattered her world.

I know exactly what she'd say if she had the chance to hand you a drink and sit with you on her back porch, because she wrote these words just months before she died. She'd look you in the eye, grab you by the shoulders, and with a smile say, "Live big. Love hard. Kiss and make up. Plant a flower. Adopt a dog. Paint something orange. Start cocktail hour a little early. Buy the convertible."[1]

Because she did.

Thrivers Aren't Superheroes

In the pages of this book you'll meet other people like Leta who somehow, despite being sucker-punched by a life they never expected, have found a way to live life to the full without waiting for rainbows and butterflies to make everything better. All of them have struggled with the lies no one's immune to, and they do their best to hold on to the truths they need to move forward. Like Leta, they are just like us. Not a superhero cape or pair of tights in sight, just a set of well-worn practices tucked in their back pocket.

Now that we've dismissed the lies for what they are and found solid ground in the truths that anchor us in the storm, let's dig into these practices. They are the key to living well whenever life falls apart, and I'm excited to dive in and begin to watch as your shoulders relax and you laugh a little more each day. But before we do, there are a few things I want you to know. They're kind of important, so lean in and listen well.

You've Got What It Takes

When we're facing down the reality of hard circumstances, it's tempting to escape into a hole or roll over and accept our new lot in life, because we just don't feel strong enough to do anything else and we've no idea which way to turn next. Pain is all-consuming. Worry is debilitating. Grief for loved ones and what-could-have-been wraps itself around us like a ten-ton blanket. Dwarfed by these mountains, it's no wonder we feel weak and powerless.

But you are stronger than you can ever imagine.

You are, friend. You are strong. You may have teeny biceps or hide your flapping bingo wings in long sleeves, and you might not be change-the-world strong, but I know for sure you *are* change-*your*-world strong. Not big, bulging Arnie or "Go ahead, make my day" strong, but small, simple "Let's go ahead and make a moment" strong.

How do I know? Because you've already taken the first small step—you've picked up this book and read this far, for starters. And you're not giving up, giving in, or going home. I know you want more, even if you're not sure what more looks like, how on God's green earth you're going to grab it, or whether you've got the strength to even take the first step. But you're here. I love that about you. Like I said, you're stronger than you think, and I'd bet my last tea bag you're braver and smarter than you know too.

You've Got the Power

How do I know you're stronger, braver, and smarter than you think? Because you're not in this alone. God sent you the Holy Spirit, your own personal Counselor, Advocate, and Comforter who's with you 24/7.

When the kids were young, my car battery died just after I'd locked and loaded three hungry, whiny under-fives into their respective car seats in my supercool mama-van. It wouldn't start. It wouldn't budge. I was stuck. I'm a pretty stubborn woman, and I was tempted to push us home, and with enough time, grit, and determination I might just have made it. But what I really needed was a fully charged battery.

Trying to jump-start our overwhelmed lives without the power of the Holy Spirit is like pushing a two-ton minivan full of screaming kids uphill, in the rain, barefoot. It might be possible, but not only is it exhausting, it's totally unnecessary when there's a free battery sitting in the boot. Even I'm not that stubborn.

We're not alone in this, and we're not limited to our own strength to do these practices. The Holy Spirit within us, whom we have access to 24/7, loves nothing more than equipping us, guiding us, comforting us, teaching us, and giving us strength, power, peace, and reassurance. It's through the Holy Spirit's power that these practices become more than just good ideas for feeling better; they become Spirit-fueled habits for living abundantly.

As a former science teacher, I love the power and simplicity of a pulley. Whether you're raising a flag, lifting a paint pot up the side of your house, or lifting a hippopotamus out of a ditch, a simple pulley lets you reverse the direction you're pulling (down, not up—so much easier) and reduce how hard you need to pull (saving those teeny biceps of ours). I know, I'm nerding out here, but finding the rubies in the rubble of our lives can feel like lifting Betty the hippo out of a ditch, and we need all the additional help we can get. Yes, we have the practices we need to do it, but God has given us the most brilliant pulley, his Holy Spirit, who makes the lifting so much easier it blows me away.

Let's not leave the Holy Spirit outside in the rain while we struggle on alone, denying ourselves his power. Why would we say "No thanks, I've got this" when we have the Creator of the universe, the Maker of the heavens and the earth, with us? We have his Son, who sees us as we reach through the crowds to touch the hem of his robe, and his Holy Spirit, who counsels, comforts, guides, and empowers us.

You might feel too weak to lift your head off the pillow, or maybe you're tempted to just give up and accept financial ruin. But with the Holy Spirit helping us each time we use one of the practices, our efforts are multiplied and life shines a little brighter. He's given us a spirit not of fear but of power, love, and self-discipline (2 Tim. 1:7). Let's use it. Let's allow it to work in us and through us and turn these practices into power practices. It's everything we need for life (2 Pet. 1:3)—a full life in him.

So Go for It

As I lay in the chemo chair, drugs that could strip paint pumping into the port just above my right boob, I'd pray for God to wave his magic wand and take it all away. He didn't, but what he did do was give me the strength to pick up my mat (John 5:8), come to him (Matt. 11:28), and push through the crowds and touch his cloak (Mark 5:27). He equipped me to step toward him and into the life he'd promised me.

Are you in? Are you willing to do the same?

Willingness is all Jesus ever asks of us. Willingness is hope, trust, faith, and action all bundled into a tentative yes. Like the distraught father who brought Jesus his demon-possessed son and pleaded, "I believe, help my unbelief!" (Mark 9:24), we can say with full confidence, "I am willing, help my unwillingness!" and he will.

Each chapter going forward covers a different practice, and in each one you'll hear from three different people: me (I know, we've already been introduced), one of my Thriver friends, and an often-forgotten woman of the Bible. Each one has used the practices in some way or another to find more when life handed them less on an empty platter. Then there's a chance for you to dig deeper in the questions, followed by a short prayer you can make your own. I'd love for you to treat this book like a workbook, highlighting bits that challenge you or stand out, scribbling notes in the margin where God nudges you with a thought, maybe chatting it through with friends you trust. Wouldn't it be great if this book was battered, bruised, and worn out from all the life you're living? I'd love that.

Remember this: those folks you see on your chemo ward, the ones who seem to have this rather disarming peace and contentment about them, or that lady at church whose laugh lights up the sanctuary as she sits with her severely disabled son—they aren't stronger, luckier, or more full of faith than you. And I'm certainly not, that's for sure.

We are just ordinary folks who've taken some practices and, with God's help, are finding the rubies in the wreckage of our crazy, messed-up-right-now lives. And you can too.

I am a Thriver.

I believe life doesn't have to be pain-free to be full.

I reject the lies of the world about who and whose I am.

I embrace the truth that I am loved, seen, and enough, and that God loves me, isn't mad, and will never leave.

I've got this because God's got me, and together we can do more than I could ever do alone.

LEARNING TO BREATHE AGAIN

You might not think you are particularly strong or brave, but I'm sure other people do. Ask a few people who know you well what they think your biggest strengths are and where they see you being brave in the midst of what you're dealing with. (You might first like to explain about this exercise so it's a little less awkward!)

How does the thought of being filled with the strength of the Holy Spirit make you feel? Excited? Nervous?

Take a moment to think about what messages you've absorbed about the Holy Spirit's role in your life and how this might affect your willingness to be open to him.

Take a moment to ask the Holy Spirit to fill you afresh or for the first time. Whether you "feel" him or not, if you ask he comes (Matt. 7:11), so take time to thank him for his presence.

Grab your calendar and block off some time every day or week to read each chapter and do the exercises, questions, and prayers. This intentional blocking off of time is a way of loving yourself, telling God you're willing, and getting the most out of the book.

Why not give yourself a little reward for completing each chapter? A bubble bath? A coffee with a friend to talk about your progress or just catch up? Setting ourselves small frequent rewards sets us up to succeed.

Dear Lord, you know more than anyone that I don't feel strong and brave. Far from it. And yet you tell me that in my weakness you are strong, and I'm so grateful for that. I need your strength every day, every minute.

Lord, I am willing to be willing. As I set off on this journey to find more of the abundant life you came to give me, fill me with your Holy Spirit and equip me with all I need.

In your name and the name of your Son, who gave his life that I might live life to the full through the power of the Holy Spirit who gives me the strength to do so. Amen.

PART 2

Learning to Breathe Again

—— 4 ——

Choose Brave

It doesn't have to be big

Healing takes courage, and we all have courage, even if we have to dig a little to find it.

Tori Amos

Have I not commanded you? Be strong and courageous. Do not be afraid; do not be discouraged, for the LORD your God will be with you wherever you go.

Joshua 1:9

Having already lost her father hours before she gave birth to her son, Becky was eight months pregnant with her daughter when her husband died.

It's true, no one gets to skip the tough stuff.

So what are we meant to do?

When I was diagnosed with rectal cancer six weeks after losing Jo, Al and I faced shattering our kids' lives all over again as we told them the news.

Life's really not fair at all.

So what are we meant to do?

Having witnessed her husband's temper and abusive ways, Abigail discovered armed men were heading toward her house (1 Sam. 25).

We can end up living a life we never signed up for.

So what are we meant to do?

Adulting isn't just hard, it has an annoying tendency to be overwhelming and life-shattering too, and when it slapped me in the face I felt frightened, out of control, and out of choices.

I like being in control—it makes me feel safe and strong. And having choices reminds me I am, despite everything, still in control, even if just by a sliver. I like to know what's coming and be the master of my own destiny, and I hate feeling like a puppet on someone else's string. But the moment I became a cancer patient, that's exactly how I felt.

Everything was laid out and decided for me: appointments, treatments, drugs, surgeries, and—thanks to an army of friends—even what we ate for dinner and how the kids got to their activities. Feeling powerless, I fixated on the few decisions I *could* make: Whether to order the mini-mega-mocha-choca or the simple cappuccino at Starbucks. Whether to splurge on those cute suede boots I'd had my eye on but absolutely did not need. Small choices like these became everything. And yes, in case you're wondering, I got the cappuccino *and* the boots.

So what are we meant to do?

It seemed like Becky, Abigail, and I were up the creek without a paddle, facing lives we hadn't signed up for and with our choices snatched from our grasp. But we did have a choice, and you do too. We can *choose brave*, and thankfully doing so doesn't require us to *be* brave, only to choose the next right thing.

Choosing brave is our first practice because it is the one that enables us to step into all the others, and thankfully brave isn't something we *are* by virtue of our inherited gene pool. It's something we *choose*, minute by minute, painful terrified step by painful terrified step. It may not be a delicious "vanilla or chocolate" kind of choice, leaving hot fudge sauce dripping through our fingers, but rather a hard "take a deep breath and brace yourself" kind of choice. But it *is* a choice, even if we have to dig a little to find the courage to make it.

Choosing Brave Is Not the Same as Being Fearless

While giving birth to her daughter Libby, Becky sobbed. In a moment meant to be filled with tears of joy and the cry of her newborn baby, her heartache collapsed in on her. Exhaustion dragged her under, and a deep longing for life to be different closed in.

Seven years earlier, Becky and Keith got engaged after meeting at church. He was the quiet, caring pastor's son. She was four years his junior and every bit as gregarious as he was unassuming. They began to hang out, discovered shared passions, started dating, and fell in love.

Two days after he popped the question, they were told Keith had anaplastic large-cell lymphoma (ALCL), a form of non-Hodgkin's lymphoma. They juggled surgery, chemo, and radiation trips with guest lists, invitations, and tuxedo fittings. Then, after a year of treatment, they tied the knot and raised their glasses to a fresh start. Newly married, with Keith's cancer behind them, Becky assumed they had survived their allotted adult crisis and looked forward to her happily ever after. Like so many of us, she couldn't have anticipated the unseen pain and loss marching unrelentingly toward her.

When Becky's father died just hours after their son Caleb was born, she says, "Anything I thought I knew about grief went straight out of the window."[1] She admits she spent the next year numb, wondering why she couldn't have her dad *and* her son, while stoically pretending life was fine.

They moved to DC, determined to make yet another fresh start, creating new memories as Caleb grew. Until Keith, now a doctor himself, began to wake at night drenched in sweat, and Becky knew something was dreadfully wrong. Perhaps the ALCL was back; they'd been told it could recur within the first five years. But just before Christmas they were given far more devastating news. It wasn't ALCL. It was another cancer—a rare, aggressive, and untreatable kind. It gave them, at best, a year together.

On New Year's Eve, just ten days after his shocking diagnosis and after a day spent treating his own patients, Keith was admitted to the hospital. Five days later he said it was time for him to go to heaven, and within an hour he was there. He hadn't even had time to start chemo.

Becky says the next month was full of anger and confusion. She knew God is sovereign, but he'd obviously stopped paying attention and had left her living a nightmare: eight months pregnant with their second child, caring for young Caleb, her heart and her life shattered.

Becky and Keith had picked out their daughter's name together: Elizabeth "Libby" Grace after Keith's grandmother and the grace God had always shown them. She came into the world just as she lives it today, kicking with energy and life.

Fast-forward a little over two years to the present as Becky and I chat on the phone, her two precious littlies chattering in the background. She is doing brilliantly. She writes and cheers on anyone setting off on a new adventure or struggling with mental health issues, and she's a wonderful mother who smiles a lot, especially when she's eating ice cream. Battling anxiety and depression, her life's not perfect and pain-free by any stretch of the imagination, but it *is* full.

When people ask her how she does it, how she's kept going, even finding joy and laughter buried in the rubble, she says she chooses brave every day. It doesn't mean she's fearless. "I'm far from it," she laughs. There's more than enough fear in her life for that. It means when faced with a choice between stepping into something hard but life-giving or taking the easier option of staying in the familiar pain of the present, she chooses to step ahead scared.

Becky reminds me of Bethany Hamilton, who triumphed in professional surfing despite losing her arm in a shark attack. Bethany says, "Courage doesn't mean you don't get afraid. Courage means you don't let fear stop you."[2] And like Bethany, Becky doesn't let her fears stop her from living her painful new life to the full.

Choosing brave is nothing new. Just as Joshua is about to lead the people of Israel into the promised land, God commands him to choose brave by stepping out in courage (Josh. 1:9). He doesn't urge him or invite him. He doesn't reason with him, arguing it would be in Joshua's best interest. He commands him and gives Joshua full assurance he will go with him.

Becky and Keith knew God would go with Becky as she journeyed on after he died. That's why Becky, like Joshua, can choose brave in the face of her daily fear, and it's why we can too.

God commands us to do the same, choosing brave for ourselves if we are to enter our own promised land—our abundant life—and we can do so knowing he will be with us whatever we face.

Choosing Brave Isn't Always Big, but It's Always Intentional

Despite feeling like a cancer puppet pulled around by bouts of nausea, a poop bag, and the never-ending rounds of doctors' offices and blood work, in reality I had to make hundreds of choices, big and small, every day. Some were important choices about my medical care. Others felt more tender, like when and how to tell my still-grieving dad and sister, or how vulnerable to be with our church. Then there were choices I had to make instantly, like whether or not to punch the lady who told me her uncle had just died a painfully agonizing death from rectal cancer. (I'll leave you guessing what I chose on that one.)

Early on, the biggest choice we faced was how to tell our kids. It loomed overhead like a piano swinging from a balcony, waiting to drop and destroy the safety of our family. The easy choice was to run from under its shadow and keep quiet, to put it off and tell them later. We knew it would freak them out. Having lost their grandma and auntie to cancer, as far as they knew people who got cancer died, and died quickly. The thought of telling them the same heat-seeking missile of death was now locked on their mum's rear end filled us with dread. Should we keep it to ourselves for a few more weeks, or maybe just tell them I'm sick but leave out the "c" word? Perhaps they're too young? But no, they weren't too young, and our family has never operated in half-truths and white lies. If we were going to get through this, we'd do it together—as Team Hardy.

Our worn and well-loved kitchen table traveled from England with us, and over the years its solid pine top has been graced with Christmas dinners, Lego castles, glitter creations, and math homework. Now, as we sat around it in our usual dinnertime places, about to share life-altering news, I was grateful to lean on its sturdy, familiar strength.

We told them doctors had found a large tumor and although they weren't certain what it was, they were pretty sure it was some kind of cancer. Until that moment, my colonoscopy—with its preparation that had confined me to within a ten-second sprint of the loo and left my insides as clean as a whistle—had been a family joke. But as we broke the news, no one laughed. We shared what we knew—the plan for radiation, chemo, and surgery—and what we didn't, what this new reality would look like and how the days ahead would unfold. Once they heard the words "mum" and "cancer" uttered in the same breath, any reassurances it wasn't the same cancer that Ma (my mum) and Auntie Jo Jo had were lost. Their mum had cancer. Period.

Sophie's voice, soft and fearful and so different from her usual boisterous confidence, broke the silence, asking the million-dollar question I hadn't even dared ask myself.

"Are you going to die, Mummy?"

Inhaling deeply, I leaned in, smiling, our brown eyes locked on one another. "Yes, darling, one day I will. But I pray not now, not from this."

I exhaled, turning my gaze to include James and Emma.

"I hope to be around for a long, long time. But whatever happens, God is good, we can trust him, and he'll be with us every step of the way."

The faith pep talk was as much for me as it was for them.

By stepping into that conversation, we set the scene for how the Hardys would roll on this one: together, with no blindfolds, work-arounds, or white lies. As hard as it was, I have no regrets. It created an environment where the kids could be honest, ask questions, and share their fears, secure in the knowledge we'd tell them the truth. It brought life into a deadly situation and drew us together rather than dividing us with the illusion of half-truths.

At the time, we didn't feel brave. We were scared—really scared. Telling them was risky. What if we were doing the wrong thing? What if they couldn't handle it and we couldn't handle their not handling it? There were no guarantees, and an easier option was there for the taking, even if we didn't believe it was a better one. It was right to tell them. Hard but right.

But isn't that always the way? The intentional, hard right choice always leads to a fuller, richer life than the one found down the easier path of least resistance. Leaving an abusive relationship, forgiving the guy who left you at the altar, seeking family counseling when you discover your teen is self-harming, or admitting your credit card debt is out of control are all brave choices. But so is going to work when your boss is a jerk, getting out of bed when your depression hits hard, showing up for a blind date because you're fed up with being single, or saying "Yes, I'll build a fort with you" when the new baby kept you up all night. These are all brave choices, friend.

Choosing brave isn't always big, but it is always intentional, and as we move ahead with intention, secure God is with us, we can steer ourselves into the abundance he has waiting for us.

Choosing Brave Is Always Worth It

Nabal was a mean, surly, brutish man, self-centered and evil in his dealings (1 Sam. 25:3) and probably far too fond of hitting the wineskin. *Nabal* means "fool" in Hebrew, and he certainly lived up to his name. Abigail was his beautiful and intelligent wife, whose name in contrast means "father's joy." Yet I can only imagine the verbal, physical, and possible sexual abuse she must have endured in this arranged marriage. She was trapped in a marriage she never agreed to, to a man she couldn't trust.

We meet this couple, as different as their names suggest, in 1 Samuel 25, when David is on the run from King Saul. While hiding in the desert, David and his men had taken care of Nabal's shepherds and their sheep. As it was now sheep-shearing time—a time marked by celebration and generosity—David sends a message to Nabal asking for special food for his men in return for their kindness. Being a mean-spirited and selfish man, Nabal refuses. In an impulsive outburst, he not only rejects the request but goes on to insult David and his men in one long, angry tirade. Equally impulsive, David retaliates by vowing to kill every male in

Nabal's household. Violence, bloodshed, and heartache seem inevitable.

I'm sure this wasn't the first time her hotheaded husband's cruel words had put Abigail in danger. We don't know how many times she'd faced the consequences of his actions before, but this time she chooses to act.

If Abigail had always followed her husband's example, taking her anger and fear out on those around her, she wouldn't have earned the trust and respect of his men and been told about the attack. Instead, by her choosing respect and kindness over judgment and anger, probably on a daily basis, Nabal's servants come to her with their news.

When she hears of the bloodshed heading toward them, Abigail has a choice: take action and risk her husband's wrath, or keep quiet and hide in fear and bitterness. Abigail chooses the brave, right thing, and while Nabal is busy stuffing his face and getting drunk, she gathers the generous gift he had refused to offer, goes out to David, and bows before him, extinguishing his burning desire to retaliate. The household is saved.

When Nabal wakes up the next morning (with what must have been one heck of a hangover) and Abigail tells him what she has done, he collapses in a fit of rage and dies ten days later. When David finds out, he asks Abigail to be his wife. Now a widow, she willingly joins him, taking her five maidservants with her.

Talk about blessings. She's no longer married to a brutish man prone to fits of rage but to David, a man after God's own heart. By choosing brave every day—from the way she treated her servants to her decision to act as peacemaker—she traded in the life she'd been surviving for a fuller, more abundant life of love, friendship, and safety.

I wish it were that easy, but it rarely is. I can't promise that by choosing brave you'll be whisked away from your terrible today into a beautiful tomorrow in the arms of a handsome man of God. But I can guarantee you that choosing brave will always produce fruit—rich, juicy fruit that will last (John 15:16)—because that is what God gives us when we remain in him.

When we lay down our hurt and fear, our unforgiveness, our desire to get even, or our need to see ourselves as a victim, we choose brave and hold up our banner of victory. It's a banner over more life, more healing, and more joy. As Lysa TerKeurst says, "It is impossible to hold up the banners of victim and victory at the same time. Our choice to give grace gives God the opportunity to step in and rewrite our story."[3] Let's give God that opportunity in our lives.

When Becky emailed me with things she wants you to know, she said this: "With every difficult situation, you have a choice: to run away or to face the hard thing. Each time you choose the brave thing and walk through the difficult situation, you are guaranteed to grow in character, find hope sooner, and experience more freedom from fear than you would have if you had avoided the struggle."[4]

She's right. By choosing brave, we choose to step away from merely surviving and walk hand in hand with God into the abundant life he has for us.

What Does Choosing Brave Look Like?

How do we make this choice toward life and away from empty survival mode? Well, so much of it depends on our willingness to trust God in the thick of it.

Becky, drowning in grief and questions, still believed God was sovereign. Somehow I knew that whether I lived or died, God was good and would be with us. Abigail, riding out to meet David without the permission of her hot-tempered and brutish husband, knew God was with David and he would do right by her (1 Sam. 25:30–33).

Brave isn't who we are or are not. We can't buy it on eBay or find an extra stash of it under the mattress. Brave is the choice we make when we come face-to-face with hard. It's what we do when we're staring down pain and heartache, our dreams are blowing away in the harsh winds of change, and we choose to step out toward life and living. It's brave because there is always an easier, safer option. It's easier to not be honest and vulnerable when we're consumed with anxiety and don't know where to turn. It's so much easier to say we're fine when we're not and to refuse help when accepting it risks admitting we're weak. But if we want to move forward in and through the raging storm our life has become, we have to step out scared.

Bravery and courage aren't reserved for soldiers, skydivers, and heroes of the faith. When life stinks so badly we need an industrial-sized air freshener just to get out of bed, bravery can be small daily acts of trust. Brave is saying "I'm having a tough day" when someone who cares asks. It's trusting God when you're still angry at him, and it's saying "I'm scared" for the first time since elementary school. It's accepting help as unreformed control freaks, and it's relaxing in a bubble bath with a large glass of wine when your to-do list is as long as a roll of toilet paper.

Choosing brave will be different for each of us, but the ripple effects of each small brave choice will travel through our storms and the darkened skies of those around us, calming the waters as they go. When Becky chooses to share her story, her vulnerability doesn't just help her process and heal; it travels far and wide, inspiring you and me to do the same. Our decision to share my diagnosis didn't save lives like Abigail's decision did, but it set in motion how we'd handle our cancer tsunami and how we'd deal with the next storm that rolled in.

Camouflaging reality with smoke and mirrors is an easier, tempting alternative for sure. Yet as we learn to walk bravely into the hard stuff, we step into a life that would otherwise elude us.

Becky doesn't regret choosing brave one bit, and nor do I. I bet Abigail didn't either, and nor will you. I don't know the specifics of your story, but I do know this: you have a spark buried deep within you crying out for more of what God has for you. Take that hunger and use it to fuel a brave choice today. I'm the one inviting you—encouraging you in my best English accent and offering all sorts of incentives— but at the end of the day, God commands you. How can you say no when he's promised to go with you?

Choosing brave is the challenging route to a full life, not the easier path to a less-than life. It's the practice we must exercise first and use most often so it gets easier to walk more fluidly through its increasingly familiar movements. Let's choose brave together.

I am a Thriver.

I believe life doesn't have to be pain-free to be full.

I reject the lies of the world about who and whose I am.

I embrace the truth that I am loved, seen, and enough, and that God loves me, isn't mad, and will never leave.

I've got this because God's got me, and together we can do more than I could ever do alone.

I choose brave, knowing it doesn't need to be big, just intentional.

LEARNING TO BREATHE AGAIN

What is causing you the most fear in your life today?

How are you responding? Are you stepping out toward those fears or hunkering down, doing your best to avoid them?

Do you feel out of control and out of choices? If so, take a good look at your life. Is that really true? List three small brave choices you could make this week.

What positive thing would happen if you stepped ahead scared and made these choices? In other words, list the upside of making these brave choices.

The Bible tells us God will be with us and never leave us (Josh. 1:9; Deut. 31:6). What specific help from God do you need as you make these brave choices today? Tell him what you need.

Now go and set a reminder on your phone or in your planner to come back and revisit this page in a week. How did it go? What was hard? What went well? What have you gained by choosing brave?

What rubies, however small, did you find when you chose brave?

Dear Lord, I get scared, terrified even. I bet you never do—you're God, after all—but I do. My fears laugh in the face of what courage I can muster and tower over any bravery I can summon. I really want to choose brave and thrive in this messy, painful time, but it's so hard. Please help me.

You say you'll be with me wherever I go, and I really need your help to do this. I need your peace when I'm afraid, your joy to lift my spirits, your wisdom to make the best decisions, and your love to tell me that, come what may, all will be well in you. All this helps me choose brave.

Thank you for being with me, however difficult things get or fearful I am. Please help this crazy truth sink deep within me so I can choose brave just as you command. Whether it's in the minutiae or the big, heavy burdens, help me be intentional and make the brave choice. Lead me to the full life you promised.

In the name of the bravest person I know, the person who chose brave to give me the full life I crave, it's in Jesus's name I pray. Amen.

—— 5 ——

Trust God

He's got impeccable credentials

When God leads us to the edge of the cliff, we can trust him and let go. One of two things will happen: either he'll catch us when we fall, or he'll teach us how to fly!

Unknown

Trust in the LORD with all your heart
   and lean not on your own understanding;
in all your ways submit to him,
   and he will make your paths straight.

Proverbs 3:5–6

There's an old story told of a young man who tripped and fell while taking an early morning walk along some clifftops and suddenly found himself hurtling toward certain death on the jagged rocks below. Halfway down he managed to grab a scrawny branch growing tenaciously on the cliff face and he clung on for dear life, dangling precariously above the raging surf. He screamed for help, but so far from the clifftop and with the roar of the crashing waves below, his shouts disappeared on the wind.

Eventually he heard a voice. "Do you need help?"

"Yes, yes, desperately. I can't hold on much longer," he shouted. "Please help me."

"I'm happy to," the voice replied calmly.

"I can't see you. Where are you?" screamed the young man, his hands about to slip.

"Oh, you can't see me. I'm God."

"Oh! OK, that's fine, I just need you to save me."

"I can do that," God assured him. "All you have to do is let go."

"What!? You want me to let go? Are you serious? I'll be smashed to smithereens on the rocks, and if that doesn't kill me, I'll drown in the crashing waves!"

"If you let go, I promise I'll save you," reiterated God, unruffled by the man's panic.

"Really?" questioned the man, his grip beginning to give way. "You'll save me if I let go?"

"Yes," God replied. "All you have to do is let go."

The man pondered silently, shifting his grip as best he could before shouting, "Is anyone else there?"

Letting Go of the Branch

When Jo's death took me to the cliff edge and my own diagnosis sent me free-falling toward the rocks below, God assured me I could trust him and let go. But trusting God when you're in free fall is deeply counterintuitive. Our reflex reaction is to reach for something, anything, and hold on for dear life, not letting go at any cost.

When life's tickety-boo and everyone's a happy camper, trusting God is a piece of cake. The sun's shining, the birds are singing, we see his smile in every sunset, and as we read the Bible his faithfulness jumps from every page. Our trust in him is so robust it's hard to believe it will ever waver, no matter what life throws our way. And that had always been my plan, to trust him no matter what.

But dangling above jagged rocks and certain death with nothing to hold on to but a struggling tree branch can change a girl's outlook faster than it takes to shout, "Look out, you're going to fall!"

American boxing champion Mike Tyson once said, "Everyone has a plan until they get punched in the mouth,"[1] and as I stared at a scan of my rear end, a tumor the size of a small planet glowing ominously from the outer orbit of my nether region, that punch hit fair and square.

How could I trust God now?

He'd promised me if I trusted him he'd make my paths straight (Prov. 3:5–6), but this was one major detour and I was speeding into oncoming traffic.

I wanted to trust him, I really did. And sometimes I did, kinda-sorta. I knew I couldn't get through without him, but letting go of the branch wasn't as easy as it looked from the safety of the clifftop. When we trust God, it's not about us and what we can do, but about him and what he can do; it's about refusing to hold on and bravely choosing to let go. So what are we meant to do when life leaves us dangling precariously like that? How do we find a way to let go of the branch, trusting all we see around us to the One we can't see beneath us?

Plan to Trust and Trust the Plan

Many moons ago, Al and I learned to scuba dive while on our honeymoon, and the instructor drilled into us day after day: plan the dive, then dive the plan. The idea being, if you plan a safe dive you'll enjoy a safe dive, no matter what emergencies come up. And along with checking our equipment meticulously and never diving alone, we stuck to this rule religiously.

One afternoon, holding our masks to our faces, we rolled off the edge of the dive boat before turning and heading toward the teeming coral below. Following our instructor, my breathing loud and steady against the swirl of the sand, I marveled at the ocean's diversity while pushing away the unnerving and unnatural realization I was breathing underwater.

He pointed to a small cave—this wasn't on the plan but we obediently followed him in, and as the darkness wrapped itself around us we could barely see each other's faces. Our instructor vanished into the darkness, leaving us alone. Pulled by the ocean's surge, unable to tell which way was up, I sucked in short, sharp, anxious breaths as we bumped into the rough cave walls.

I grabbed Al's arm, pulled him closer until our masks almost touched, and shook my head, my eyes wide with fear. Holding hands, we turned to get the heck out of there. We didn't see our instructor again until we took long, welcome breaths of the salty, tropical air at the surface. I was mad.

Why did he go into the cave? What happened to "plan the dive, then dive the plan"?

When we get the call telling us the biopsy is malignant or we discover our middle schooler is being cyberbullied, we need a plan to trust God, because it's at these moments we lose all logical reasoning and everything in us wants to grip tighter and not let go. When life leaves me dangling on a cliff edge or gasping for air in the inky blackness of one of life's caves, good intentions left over from easier days don't cut it. My default isn't to look up, let go, and place all my fear, anger, pain, and unknowns in his hands. It's just not. So I need a plan.

For me, that plan must be tangible, practical, step-by-step, and implementable. A general one-step plan to "trust in the Lord" isn't enough when I can't breathe and *do not want* to trust.

I need to plan to trust, then trust the plan.

Here is my five-step plan. I use it pretty much every day, and it's super simple because simple is what we need most at times like this.

1. Check God's credentials.
2. Ask him for help.
3. Choose to hold on.
4. Let go.
5. Keep a record.

Check God's Credentials

Five years down the line and cancer-free, I had to stop seeing my oncologist and find myself a primary care doctor.

I loved my oncologist and felt safe with her, so it felt like she was breaking up with me. But I did what women do whether we need a new doctor or a new outfit—I asked my girlfriends. Who did they go to? Did they like them? Were they a good doctor? Then I checked their background and read reviews online. No one hires a plumber without checking their credentials, and I certainly wasn't going to trust a doctor without finding out if she's legit and has a heart as well as a brain (trust me, I've met doctors with only the latter).

Isn't it the same with God? If we're going to trust him with our lives and everything we hold close, shouldn't we check out his credentials to see if he's up to the job? We just need to know where to find them.

We can check out how many five-star ratings he has by reading stories of his faithfulness in the Bible, asking friends with uncannily high levels of trust in God, and diving into biographies of people who've trusted him through unspeakable hardship. Then we ask: Does God have a good track record? Is he trustworthy?

Digging into Bible stories of normal everyday people— like the Israelites who wandered the desert for forty years, Ruth who lost all the men in her life, Mary Magdalene, or the woman at the well—I see women who chose to trust God and saw him answer their prayers, not always in ways they expected but always for their best. These stories build my trust levels because they tell me he's been trustworthy many times before.

I asked a friend who had lived through financial pressures, job losses, and two of her four kids being diagnosed with learning difficulties how she could continue to trust God. She told me she couldn't not trust. He'd come through so many times in so many beautiful and unexpected ways, to not trust would be absurd. Absurd—that's what she called not trusting God. That's quite a five-star review.

If I need further evidence or a boost to my trust levels, I read the thrilling biographies of godly men and women throughout history who've endured relentless hardship, persecution, or suffering but have seen God come through on his promises so often they can't not trust him either. Joni Eareckson Tada, Jackie Pullinger, Corrie ten Boom, Kara Tippetts—these are just a handful of the women whose stories of trusting God through insurmountable heartache and pain have strengthened my trust.

Marshall McCluhan, the Canadian philosopher and intellectual, is famous for saying, "We drive into the future using only our rearview mirror."[2] When we check out God's credentials, we march into our future focused on his past faithfulness, building our trust and raising our expectations that he will fulfill his promises.

Ask Him for Help

On a gap year after university, I jumped off a platform 150 feet above a small pond with nothing but an oversized rubber band around my ankles. Yes, I went bungee jumping.

While I waited my turn, people jumped into free fall with varying degrees of bravado before being caught by the elastic (at what seemed like the last moment), only to bounce skyward again. Like a runaway rubber ball, they ricocheted up and down until they finally came to a stop.

No one had fallen. No one had died. The rubber band hadn't slipped off anyone's ankles, and people screamed with raw delight. But as I perched on that little platform, the dinghy below now toy-sized, I froze. There was no way I was launching myself headfirst into the void.

I asked Pete, the disarmingly handsome chap who'd just strapped my ankles together, if he could help—you know, maybe give me a mighty shove? Unfortunately, that was against the rules, but as I hopped to the edge I saw him wink cheekily and felt his big rugged hand hover inches from my back. Leaning close, his breath on my neck, he bellowed, "Three, two, one . . . GO!" Without a second thought I obeyed and dived off, screaming with a giddy cocktail of terror and joy topped off with a large dash of adrenaline.

I loved it. I absolutely loved it. I still talk about it thirty years later (yes, thirty, but who's counting?). But I would never have done it without Pete's help. I didn't have the capacity to jump alone.

Like Pete, God won't push us. Trust that's not freely given isn't trust but manipulation, and he loves us too much for that. And yet he's so keen to help, he sent us his Holy Spirit, and we need only ask. Jesus tells us, "How much more will your Father in heaven give [the help of] the Holy Spirit to those who [just] ask him" (Luke 11:13).

In the darkness of cancer, not having the strength or often the desire to trust, I had to ask for his help. Falling into the abyss of chemo nausea or waiting on scan results, I'd pray, "Help me. I believe; help my unbelief. I trust; help me trust. Give me courage to trust you." He never said no. Not once. I'd feel his hand gently rest on my back and hear him cheering me while the Spirit boosted my courage enough to jump.

If you're struggling to trust God today, please ask him for help. He will help you. He loves you too much not to.

When we're willing to be willing, taking a step toward our Father and saying, "I trust; help my lack of trust," he smiles and says, "I'd love to" before filling us with his Spirit and placing our hand in his.

Choose to Hold On

When she was fourteen, with the awkwardness of middle school nearly behind her and the freedom of high school on the horizon, Grace fell during a cheerleading stunt. While looking for signs of a concussion, doctors found a benign tumor at the base of her brain, and as she continued to grow so did the tumor. When Grace stopped growing the tumor didn't, so by the time she was twenty-one it affected her vision, dexterity, and balance, and as an emerging artist it was devastating. To this day Grace is often bedridden by the daily headaches from the constantly growing, inoperable tumor inside her head.

To combat the tumor's growth Grace has endured five—yes, five—brain surgeries: one to combat the tumor's growth and four to sort out complications from the tumor itself. The first four operations were in the space of one year; the fifth and final one was just a few months before she walked down the aisle. This girl knows about pain. This beautiful young artist knows what it's like to have pain painted over every inch of your life until you're backed into a corner screaming for mercy. She knows what it is to fear never growing old as she hears the empty echo of unanswered prayers only interrupted by the roar of the lie that it's all her fault.

How in the name of all things good and fair does she carry on, let alone hold on and trust God? I needed to know. I wanted to drink the magic "trust God in all things" potion she must sip with her morning tea.

Unfortunately, there's no magic potion, and Grace is the first to admit trusting God is an ongoing battle and a choice she has to make daily. She understands having a brain tumor isn't her choice but knows trusting God *is*, saying, "I choose to trust day in, day out that good is coming." This is what she chooses to hold on to.

In fact, "good is coming" has become her rally cry. This simple yet powerful battle call spurs her to hold on to what she knows to be true about God, who she is in him and to him, and what he has for her, even in her darkest moments. She's inspired by George MacDonald's words: "Yet I know that good is coming to me—that good is always coming; though few have at all times the simplicity and the courage to believe it."[3] Grace says, "Hope is integral to our faith as believers in Christ, and holding on to hope is not easy but is ultimately what keeps us going when the days are long, the circumstances don't make sense, and the pain feels overwhelming."[4] She's able to hold on because she's checked him out, found him trustworthy, and asked for his help a thousand times over. She then chooses to cling to who and what she knows to be true rather than to her pain and fear. She's never regretted it.

Like Grace, I didn't choose to have cancer, and I bet you didn't choose the junk you're battling right now. But friend, we can choose to hold on. We may feel powerless, but we're not. This choice to trust God is still firmly ours. Once we choose to trust God more than we trust the lies, pain, and ourselves, we see he is unshakable. Trusting God doesn't just happen the moment we meet Jesus; it's a daily choice as we face the world head-on. Will you make that choice with me?

Let Go

When I was nine months pregnant with our third child and the size of an SUV, I was desperate to meet the little person who woke me each night by jumping on my bladder. It was all so exciting despite having done it twice before.

As Jochebed carried her third child, the people of Israel were enduring the tyranny of Egypt's pharaoh (Exod. 1–2), and so I'm sure she felt only a fraction of the excitement she had while pregnant with Miriam and Aaron. What if this baby was a boy? Afraid of the Israelites' increasing numbers and having failed to quash their growth, Pharaoh had resorted to mass genocide, ordering that all Hebrew baby boys be thrown into the Nile (Exod. 1:22). Like every Hebrew exiled and enslaved in Egypt, Jochebed was painfully aware a boy would be in grave danger and her time with this little person would soon come to a devastating end.

The moment Jochebed knew she had a son, his death must have seemed inevitable. As she lifted her precious baby into her arms and breathed in his wet, milky smell, her maternal heart must have shattered. What could she do? There seemed no way out.

I've had three babies and know babies cry (a lot), and yet Jochebed managed to keep Moses hidden for three months until she couldn't hide him any longer. Then, in faith, she set her precious cargo adrift in the waters of the Nile (Heb. 11:23). She had no idea if he'd live or die, but she let go.

The rest, as they say, is history. Pharaoh's daughter spotted the basket, sent her slave to snatch it from the waters, and took pity on the Hebrew baby boy inside. Moses's sister,

Miriam, was waiting nearby and asked Pharaoh's daughter if she'd like someone to nurse the baby for her, then fetched her mother. Jochebed not only saved the life of her son but got to love, feed, and nurture him before he was eventually adopted by Pharaoh's daughter.

To give Moses a chance at life, Jochebed had to let go of him and what little control she still had. She had to let go of her son in order to hold on to her God.

We can't stay in control *and* want God to be in control. All too often we trust ourselves way too much and trust God not nearly enough. We have to pick one. To trust God fully we must let go fully. Trust isn't trust if it's incomplete. We can't set our precious cargo adrift on the river of faith and tie a rope to it just in case.

Perhaps you need to let go of control, or maybe what you need to release is worry, unforgiveness, what other people think of you, or your own ability to fix things. For me it was a whole lot of everything.

The real question is, How do we let go? I know it's easier said than done, and I've found that it helps to think of letting go and holding on as one complete action. I can't hold God's promises if my hands and heart are full of the fear of my cancer returning.

When I woke in the hospital's dim light the night after my first surgery and realized I was lying in a pool of blood, I rang for the nurse as image after image flooded my mind. I received my medical degree at the college of *Grey's Anatomy*, so I knew pools of blood are rarely good news and I began to panic. All I had the capacity to do was breathe in Jesus and breathe out the fear. I even pictured it in my mind:

Breathe in the peace of Jesus, breathe out the fear.

Hold on to Jesus, let go of the fear.

Hold on to his promise, let go of control.

Trusting God is simultaneously a letting go of what we think will make everything better and a holding on to the promise that with him everything *is* better.

Keep a Record

Despite writing a book, I'm not much of a writer, and I keep prayer journals more sporadically than I like to admit. Over the years, these intermittent ramblings and cries for help have added up, and looking back they read like a balance sheet with only credits where God has been faithful: my needs met, my longings filled, my fears soothed, and my hopes lifted. I see the God who loves me enough to read my journal (boy, he's brave), and as the pages turn I watch his faithfulness, love, and mercy unfold, not always as expected but always in love. Reading it is like thirstily guzzling a "Trust Gatorade." My trust is replenished and fortified, my hope is strengthened, and I'm ready to get back in the game of life.

My friend Grace does this too. She writes down answers to prayer whether they're big, small, or in-between. She says she doesn't just wait for the big stuff. "The big stuff isn't enough to sustain our hope. When there's more [on the list], the pattern of God showing up time and time again is more helpful than one big thing I can just explain away."[5]

The Old Testament version of a journal was an altar. Read any story of God's faithfulness, provision, and general miracle-working awesomeness, and at the end you'll see the people building an altar to God and naming the place after what he's done. I love this. It acts as a permanent reminder of his past faithfulness that builds their trust in his present and future faithfulness.

Becoming altar builders gives us somewhere to go to check God's credentials, and so our trust is built again and the cycle continues. Evidence of past trustworthiness builds strong foundations for future trust, and by keeping a record we lay that foundation one stone at a time.

Walking through grief and cancer has taught me so much about trusting God, but I admit it's still a struggle. I have to plan to trust and trust the plan if I'm going to get my stubborn butt out of the driver's seat and let him drive. I'm grateful that, in the words of Erin Brown Hollis, "He happens to be available whenever we need him. His schedule is never too busy. His phone lines are never tied up. He even works nights and weekends."[6] And he has proved he is worthy of our trust.

I am a Thriver.

I believe life doesn't have to be pain-free to be full.

I reject the lies of the world about who and whose I am.

I embrace the truth that I am loved, seen, and enough, and that God loves me, isn't mad, and will never leave.

I've got this because God's got me, and together we can do more than I could ever do alone.

I choose brave, knowing it doesn't need to be big, just intentional.

I trust God, even when I don't want to and can't sense
his presence, because I've checked his credentials
and can let go of everything I've been clinging to.

LEARNING TO **BREATHE AGAIN**

Check out God's credentials by reading the story of Joseph
in Genesis 37–47. How did God prove himself trustworthy
to Joseph?

Describe a time when you have seen God show up in your
life. If you're not sure he has, don't just think about whether
he's been there in life-altering moments but think back to
whether you've seen him in smaller, more personal ways.

Write a prayer asking for God's help to trust him. You can
make this one your own if you like: "I'm struggling to trust
you, God. I'm worried about _____,
I'm frightened _____ will happen, and
_____ is so painful I can hardly
breathe. Trusting you is hard because of all this and I'm

_____ [how you're feeling: scared, alone, etc.]. Please fill me with your Holy Spirit and give me the courage and strength to let go and trust you. Amen."

Which promise of God do you most need to hold on to right now?

His presence forever (Deut. 31:8)

His peace (Phil. 4:7)

His comfort (Isa. 49:13)

His provision (2 Cor. 9:8; Phil. 4:19)

His strength (Isa. 41:10)

His unconditional love (John 3:16)

His forgiveness (1 John 1:9)

He will fight for you (Exod. 14:14)

He will work all this for your good (Rom. 8:28)

He has good plans for you (Jer. 29:11)

Take a moment to write out that Scripture and put it somewhere you'll see it every day. Memorize it, turning it into your battle cry.

What do you need to let go of in order to fully grab hold of God? Fear? Worry? Control? Unforgiveness? Grief? Something else? Take a moment somewhere quiet to breathe in your battle cry and breathe out everything you need to let go of. Repeat it over and over, slowing your breath with each cycle.

Start to build altars by keeping notes in your journal of how God meets your needs, calms your anxiety, brings hope through a friend, or proves himself trustworthy in any way.

If you write a prayer journal, reread its pages, marking where God has met you in the past.

Make a list of how God has been present to you over the last few months, continuing to add to it as you hold on and trust him in the months ahead.

Dear Lord, thank you for never leaving me or turning your back on me when I struggle to trust you. I'm glad your track record is so robust, because in my pain I need extra reassurance you'll do what you say. Sorry, it's just hard right now. I want to trust you. Help my lack of trust.

Some things are so precious that I'm frightened to let go of them and entrust them to someone else—even you. Help me release them, placing them in your safe hands, knowing you've got this, you've got me, and you've got the people I love most in this world. Help me hold on to you; after all, you are the Rock.

Lord, as I trust you more, show me more of who you are and the full life you promised me. I want to fill up journals with the stories of how amazing you are. I want my trust to grow and strengthen. I trust; help my lack of trust.

In your name, the name that is trustworthy beyond all others. Amen.

6

Find Community

Thriving is a team sport

Call it a clan, call it a network, call it a tribe, call it a family. Whatever you call it, whoever you are, you need one.

Jane Howard

By yourself you are unprotected.
With a friend you can face the worst.
Can you round up a third?
A three-stranded rope is not easily snapped.

Ecclesiastes 4:12 MSG

I didn't want to judge the poor woman. She seemed nice enough. It's just that she had absolutely no idea I wasn't who she thought I was. I don't mean she thought I was someone else entirely. She just had me pegged all wrong.

I'd had an appointment with her on my calendar since the week I was diagnosed, and my chart sat like a ticking bomb on the table between us. All she knew about me was in that chart: *Hardy, Nicola. Female. 44 years old. ypT3 pN1 M0 Rectal Adenocarcinoma*. All I knew about her was that she was my cancer navigator and her name was Darcy.

Her role, as her title suggested, was to help me navigate my cancer journey, and if I needed anything I could call her and she'd help or find someone who could. I liked Darcy. She was smart, funny, down to earth, and had a love of English TV, which is always a winner. She saw me as a person, not as a cancer statistic or a problem to be solved. We clicked immediately except for her annoying thing about "community." She gushed endlessly about how helpful it would be to meet complete strangers (who I had nothing in common with except similarly placed tumors) to chat about how messed up and nauseous our lives had become (my words not hers, of course).

I'd told her quite emphatically I was fine—I didn't want or need to join a group, belong to a support system, or discover the joys of group counseling—but at each appointment she kept at it. Like a high-end personal shopper tasked with finding the perfect outfit, she was relentless in her calm, patient manner. I fought back equally calmly but not quite so patiently.

Week after week the conversation repeated itself in the same rhythmic dance. I admired her perseverance, yet in spite of her encouragement, I actively avoided the cancer community. All that caring, sharing, ribbon-wearing kumbaya stuff filled me with the heebie-jeebies. I'd cope alone, thanks all the same.

The trouble was, that's all I did: cope. Without a community sailing the same cancer-infested waters as I was, and holding back some of my deepest fears from close friends, I began to feel lonely and unseen, despite everyone cheering me on and helping in a million different ways. I discovered the danger of coping alone is we end up wandering lonely in a crowd.

The Community Conundrum

When life's easy and we're happy hamsters, community is fun and hassle-free, but as soon as that changes we shrink back. We yearn for connection with all its richness, yet at our most raw and vulnerable, and needing that richness more than ever, we avoid it, protecting ourselves from possible further damage. I call this the "community conundrum."

Part of Us Craves Community

God is community. He's not just community minded or a fan of community living. He *is* community—three persons in one. It's who he is by his nature and at his core.

We, dear friend, are "marvelously made" (Ps. 139:14 MSG). Not because of our stunning good looks or witty personalities but because God knitted us together in his image (Gen. 1:27) and didn't make a mistake. Since we reflect his likeness, we too, at our core, are made for community. Every single one of us. Even me, the Cope-Alone Ranger.

Community is God's plan for his people. It always has been and always will be, and we can see the life-giving thread of community permanently woven through the pages of the

Bible. Our ache for connection comes from our heavenly Father in the same way my Roman nose comes from my earthly father (sorry, Dad!), and in satisfying this craving we ultimately find more life. It's a genius move if we don't dig in our heels and reject it all, because the act of connecting human to human in this disconnected world does more than connect us to a person. It connects us to the person of God.[1]

Ask a Norwegian why they are so happy and they reply with a "we" as opposed to an "I" statement.[2] That's because, as research shows us, a full life doesn't need to be pain-free but *does* need to be lived in community. The annual World Happiness Report even uses a country's level of social support as one of its seven measures of how happy its residents can be. When a sense of community is strong, health and wealth take on less importance.

Interacting person to person bolsters our immune system, sends feel-good hormones surging through our bloodstream to our brains, and helps us live longer.[3] Sharing about our pain (physical or emotional) even reduces the number of pain receptors that are stimulated, so our pain level actually goes down.[4] As we gather in groups with similar experiences, we create a shared sense of identity and a brighter future.[5] In other words, hope. As author Kristen Strong says, "My ability to accept and thrive through change is directly proportional to the state of my near and dear friendships."[6] The benefits of community are almost endless.

God, who is community, made us for community. We have a community-shaped hole within us and yearn for it to be filled, and by bravely allowing others in we free ourselves to experience more of his full life.

And Yet Part of Us Avoids Community

I'm an extrovert who's never met a silence she can't fill, a people person who at the end of a long day will say, "I'm pooped, let's go to that party." Before I was sick my focus was often outward—arms wide open to exploring new connections and deepening old ones. I wasn't a community-loving, knit-your-own-granola, commune-living hippie type, but I valued and loved the people around me and found it easy. My community-shaped hole was full and life was good, but having cancer shut down that part of me. I closed ranks, too tired and vulnerable to let anyone in.

If we're made for community and it's an important ingredient for living fully (whether life's a bed of roses or a pile of manure), why do we avoid it like pubescent boys avoid personal hygiene whenever a manure pile lands on our doorstep? In a nutshell, because when we need it most, community feels too hard and too high risk.

Even if you're not quite so community phobic as I was, you may feel similar pangs of nervousness at the thought of diving into community right now.

Here are my top seven reasons for avoiding community when I first got cancer.

I was scared. What if they didn't like me? What if they expected intimacy and vulnerability? I don't do emotions. They are raw, scary things I can't control.

I was arrogant. I assumed these folks couldn't teach me anything I didn't already know or that I couldn't ask Google, a doctor, or Darcy.

I didn't want to get hurt again. I'd lost Mum and Jo and didn't want to risk getting close to a bunch of cancer patients who were more likely to pop their clogs than your average Joe.

I was in denial. I didn't want to admit I was "one of them"—a cancer patient.

I was wary. I'd been burned and rejected by being vulnerable in community in the past. I wanted to protect myself.

I was proud. I believed the lie that support groups are for the weak and feeble—people who can't cope alone. I was strong, I had this, and I didn't need others.

I was selfish. I had limited time and energy and needed to spend it on me, my family, and getting well. I couldn't be weighed down by other people's problems.

Ouch, right?

Please don't beat yourself up if you see yourself in here. It's understandable given what you're going through. Of course you want to protect yourself; the world hasn't protected you. Of course you're scared; you've been ripped apart and left raw and vulnerable. Of course you don't want to get hurt again. I get it.

When life is at its toughest, community seems like a high-risk investment.

In a world that values the "self-made person," the "make-it-happen captain," and a "positive mental attitude," it's unsurprising we hide when we're none of these. But steering away from community in an act of self-preservation drives away the love, support, and connection God offers. I began to realize I needed community, and by stubbornly standing alone on the outside looking in I was rejecting all it offered me.

Created with a community-shaped hole within us, we need and crave community. And yet when life is hardest and we need it most, we shy away. Here, at the end of ourselves, community—in all its wonderful, life-giving messiness—is often more than we can cope with. So we go it alone, only to crave connection more as this hole grows deeper.

There you have it, the community conundrum in all its full-life-limiting glory. We desire community and avoid it, love it and hate it, need it desperately and fearfully shun it. Together we must solve this conundrum, break the cycle, and be set free from these paralyzed places.

Learn to Dance in Community

Like a hedgehog poked with a stick, I had rolled into a ball of prickles. I was safe but alone. As I began to uncurl and realize safe isn't always where the life is, I began to first step into the community already around me and then out toward a new community I went in search of. I like to think I danced my way there: step in, step out, step in, step out. As we step to the beat of our hearts yearning for connection, we discover community isn't so high risk after all.

Step In to Those around You

As I unfurled, I saw others waiting for me. All I had to do was stop turning away and step in toward them. It wasn't a physical step but an emotional one—a step of the heart, which for me was far more difficult.

The women who traveled with Jesus knew how to step in with their hearts, not just their feet. They were people just like us—hurting, healing, looking for more than their current lives and tangible pain offered. There was Mary Magdalene, Joanna, Susanna, Mary the mother of James, Salome, and the mother of the sons of Zebedee, along with others whose names and stories we'll never hear.[7] They had found all they ached for in Jesus so they followed him, not wanting the source of their newfound life to move on without them.

These women weren't just hangers-on, mere Jesus groupies eager for the next Instagram-worthy miracle. This was an intimate group of capable women, some of whom had defied social expectations to marry and bear children in order to follow, serve, and provide for this itinerant rabbi's ministry. Each one had her own story—a story that found fullness in Jesus.

As they prepared meals together, traveled the dusty roads side by side, and discussed Jesus's teachings, I imagine them sharing their stories: where they'd come from, what they'd endured, and how they ached for more. Each conversation a step deeper into connection and community. As night fell I'm sure they smiled and laughed like any group of like-minded women sharing life and wine together.

They were family, a tribe, a clan. They set out to follow Jesus and stepped into community along the way. Coming together was unplanned; staying together was deliberate.

These women may have found themselves together by chance, but as they shared life and eventually Jesus's death and resurrection, they chose to step in toward each other with intention, going beyond the mundane and superficial. That's the scary step of the heart I'm talking about. To step in, we must unfurl our protected hedgehog bodies and dare to show each other our unprotected emotions.

Our unintentional communities are the connections and friendships that grow organically around the school gates, at the gym, and around the coffee machine at work. They are the people we sit beside at church each week, our neighbors, and our friends and family, the people life has connected us to. This community may be unintentional, but to gather its riches we must step into it with intention.

Now don't get me wrong and start panicking. I'm not asking you to shock the postman with the intimate details of your colonoscopy or tell the barista at Starbucks about the darkest moments of your IVF treatment. I'm simply suggesting we step out of the shadows and let ourselves—our real selves—be seen.

My girlfriends rallied with the speed of an emergency crash team when I told them I had cancer, and the more honest and open I became the greater the jolt of life I received.

Eventually I had to tell people outside our immediate friends and family that I had cancer—and not just any cancer but rectal cancer. The trouble was, I didn't look sick. During treatment I never lost my hair, and my chemo comfort foods were bagels and buns, so I wasn't your stereotypical pale, bald, underweight cancer patient. I'd also just run a marathon, so when I told people they were utterly shocked. I remember telling the mum of one of our kid's friends. I didn't want to tell her—all my pride, arrogance, and fear of vulnerability clouded the waters. But as I stepped down the garden path to where she waited to whisk the kids off to practice, I braced myself and gave her the news. She was shocked, yes, but more than that, as the wall I'd built around me cracked, she really saw *me*, maybe for the first time. Her mama heart broke for mine, and from then on, whenever she drove the kids, we didn't skirt around superficial mum talk but marched right through the door I'd just opened to each other's lives.

A few weeks later I nervously stepped in again and accepted our prayer team's offer to pray for healing. It's one thing to admit you're not a perfect pastor's wife, but it's another thing entirely to accept the laying on of hands for a tumor lodged in your backside. Yet this generous and intimate shared act of faith is still producing the fruit of community in all our lives today.

Stepping in required me to let go of who I thought I should be and how I wanted others to see me, and to be who I really am, which Brené Brown assures us is essential for connection.[8] Stepping deeper into the connections already around me may have been uncomfortable, but it took them to a fresher, deeper, more fulfilling place.

As those women looked up at Jesus, beaten and flogged, breathing his last on the cross, their world shattered. They had found life in this man and now he was dying. Despite the suffocating weight of grief and confusion, none of them turned away to cope alone. Instead, they stepped further in, wrapping their arms around each other, holding one another up. Three days later they went to the tomb and found it empty, and finding Jesus alive they celebrated together.

Stepping into community in our pain provides a readymade party when it's time to celebrate.

Step Out and Find Your "I Get It" Tribe

Maggie had her first seizure just after her first birthday. Her mum, Erin, was about to take little Maggie and her older brother, Anderson, outside to play when Maggie fell to the floor, limp, and shook violently before she stopped breathing and started turning blue. Erin, pregnant with her third child, had no idea her daughter was having her first epileptic seizure.

As the paramedics raced to their quiet cul-de-sac, Erin placed her mouth over her daughter's and started rescue breathing. She had never seen a seizure before, but as more seizures followed in the weeks ahead she became all too familiar with the fear and helplessness that surrounds them.

When Maggie's little sister, Ellie, was born, it took just eighteen months before she too had a seizure. Having three kids under five is tough enough for any mum, but two of Erin's three kids were epileptic toddlers. The mum life she'd dreamed of vanished and was replaced by a new normal filled with uncertainty, helplessness, and guilt. She was drowning in questions and feeling hopeless.

Despite having friends and family who loved her well, folded laundry, and babysat so she could nap, Erin still felt isolated. No one she knew had kids with epilepsy, let alone two toddlers eighteen months apart. She needed others to say, "Me too . . . I get it." Craving mums who could empathize, not just sympathize, she bravely stepped out to find them.

In online support groups and on websites about epilepsy she found the emotional, practical, and spiritual help and connection she so desperately needed. She found other mums who understood, wanted to journey with her, and affirmed that her current reality was worthy of mourning. She was given helpful, practical advice, such as to always be prepared for the unexpected by packing a bag of seizure supplies, and was then encouraged to go and live her life and not be trapped at home by the fear of a seizure happening in public. This community became such a place of hope and peace that when Maggie had a seizure after being seizure-free for five years, it was this community that Erin turned to. These were the friends who could help her mourn, understand when she screamed, "I thought it was over!" and allow her to feel her pain in a safe space.

Erin had found true friends. With her world in tatters, she'd gone hunting for help and understanding and found friendship and community. She intentionally stepped out to look for what she didn't have.

I hope you've got a tremendous gaggle of friends and family who are loving you, holding you, making you tea, and wiping your tears, but if they don't truly understand what you're going through, please step out and find your people. It doesn't negate your family's role or mean your friends aren't good enough; it just means you have needs they can't meet. And that's okay. Al didn't know what it felt like when my ostomy bag leaked in Target, and it wasn't fair for me to expect him to. We all need people who can say, "I get it. I understand."

By stepping into "I get it" spaces, we break the community conundrum and find connection with people who've been where we are, allowing them into our darkest places.

Finding More Than Community in Community

Made in the image of the God who is community, we will always long for the connection and fullness it brings; but when life is painful and finding community seems the hardest, we only taste a fraction of it if we turn away in self-protection.

We can find the abundant life God promised us amongst today's tears, but not as a Cope-Alone Ranger. Darcy was right after all—thriving *is* a team sport.

I am a Thriver.

I believe life doesn't have to be pain-free to be full.

I reject the lies of the world about who and whose I am.

I embrace the truth that I am loved, seen, and enough, and that God loves me, isn't mad, and will never leave.

I've got this because God's got me, and together we can do more than I could ever do alone.

I choose brave, knowing it doesn't need to be big, just intentional.

I trust God, even when I don't want to and can't sense his presence, because I've checked his credentials and can let go of everything I've been clinging to.

I lean into community because thriving is a team sport and no one wins alone.

LEARNING TO BREATHE AGAIN

Which of my reasons for avoiding community that I listed on pp. 103–4 do you resonate with most and why?

Make a list of friends, family, and unintentional community, then write their names in concentric circles (similar to the figure below) based on how safe and connected to them you feel, with the most intimate relationships in the center. Does anyone's position surprise you? How might you step into these relationships more intentionally and get the help, support, or friendship you need?

Relationship Circle

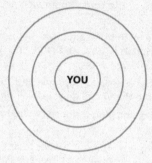

Where can you find others who are dealing with the same issues as you? Can you reach out to at least one person or group this week?

Oh dear Lord, thank you for being community and for not creating me to live alone. Thank you for the DNA running deep within me that thrives on relationships, shared experiences, and love.

I'm sorry for the times I've rejected your hands and feet who have come to hold me and walk with me. Forgive my arrogance and selfishness. Forgive my fear and trembling. Keeping my head above water is lonely, and I know I can't thrive alone. I need community, I want community, but community can be scary and intimidating, Lord.

Show me who my tribe is and help me step in through the doors of the community you have prepared for me. When I'm closed off to people who want to love me, open my heart, and when I avoid people because of my mess and pain, give me courage to embrace them. As I step out to find my "I get it" community, give me eyes to see where you're leading, strength to be myself, and openness to receive all you have for me.

Lord, thank you for not leaving me alone, for being with me and providing friends, family, and community. In your precious name, the name that by its nature is community—Three in One. Amen.

7

Be Vulnerable

Stiff upper lips need ChapStick

Vulnerability sounds like truth and feels like courage. Truth and courage aren't always comfortable, but they're never weakness.[1]

Brené Brown

But he said to me, "My grace is sufficient for you, for my power is made perfect in weakness." Therefore I will boast all the more gladly about my weaknesses, so that Christ's power may rest on me.

2 Corinthians 12:9

Cancer wasn't going to quit so neither could I. If only one of us could survive, I had to put on my big-girl undies, wax my stiff upper lip, and do what I do best—stay strong. Cancer had met its match.

In my small, stubborn mind, staying strong enabled me to protect our kids from seeing their mum weak, in pain, and quite possibly dying. Wasn't that my job as mama bear, to protect her cubs? I could also shield Al from the fear keeping me awake at night and the sight of his wife too weak to walk to the loo. He was carrying enough already and didn't need me hitching a ride. Subconsciously it protected me too. The stronger I acted, the stronger I felt. And surely the stronger I felt, the less damage cancer could do, right?

The trouble was, as I battened down the hatches I became cold. I lost my softness, my lightness, and even my ridiculous sense of humor. I couldn't keep scary emotions boxed away without numbing the life-giving ones, and I slowly closed down, turning in, shying away. Perhaps I was inadvertently preparing those I love for the worst; if I was coldhearted, maybe it wouldn't be so devastating for them if I didn't make it.

The trouble is, when you batten down the hatches, it's too dark to see the rubies in the rubble.

Our Strength Can Be Our Biggest Weakness

It turns out my strength was my biggest weakness, nearly destroying our marriage in its wake.

Don't get me wrong, there's definitely a time and place for taking a deep breath and harnessing your inner strength, and it might be the only thing holding your life together, getting you out of bed to fix lunch for your kids or showing up to your doctor's office. But by pitching my tent in Camp

Strong, I eventually took up permanent residence and forgot my way home.

"Fake it till you make it" might work when we walk into a room of unknown faces or start a job feeling like an imposter, but it's an empty falsehood to live by permanently. A month or so into treatment, I had managed to convince both Al and myself that I was doing just fine. Believing my Oscar-worthy performance, he gave me the space he assumed I craved. But I was far from okay. I desperately needed a hug from arms I could collapse into without fear of judgment. I needed to share the emotional weight I was lugging around, and I needed to be understood, accepted, and loved, even if I was undone and broken. I just didn't know how and couldn't bring myself to try.

Poor Al couldn't win. He took care of the kids and held our lives together (while also running CityChurch) as I focused on scan appointments, chemo regimens, and which herbal tea didn't make me want to vomit. It wasn't that he wasn't interested—he was, deeply. But I kept telling him I was fine and pushed him away, so he sweetly left me alone. When my warped brain told me this meant he didn't care, I kept to myself even more, telling him again and again I was okay, and so the beat went on. Slowly we began to drift dangerously apart.

It turns out I was more afraid of losing Al than of sharing my emotions. Not knowing what else to do, I exploded in an emotional avalanche. All my hidden fears, hurts, and assumptions that he didn't care sheared off my mountain of strength, nearly burying the poor man. He never saw it coming. But as the more empathetic and emotionally intelligent one in our marriage, rather than fighting his way up to the surface he dug down to me and helped me breathe.

Ironically, when we share our pain it actually hurts less. Research tells us when our vulnerability is met with empathy we feel less pain, emotional or physical,[2] enabling us to open ourselves to the love and belonging we're gasping for. The trouble was, my strength had slammed the door on vulnerability like a fuming teenager shuts out her parents. It might have felt good for a moment, but it didn't solve anything and eventually made things worse. Brené Brown says, "Authenticity is a collection of choices that we have to make every day. It's about the choice to show up and be real. The choice to be honest. The choice to let our true selves be seen."[3] I'd been anything but authentic. I hadn't shown up day by day, little by little, and had lost out on so much as a result.

Please don't make the same mistake I did. Letting yourself be seen as you navigate your way through this will help you breathe deeper than I ever could dressed in my suffocating, skin-tight superhero outfit.

Learn to Walk in Vulnerability

Mary and Martha's brother was sick and dying. They had sent word to Jesus that his friend was gravely ill, but he never showed up and now Lazarus was dead. No wonder Martha was mad (John 11).

So many mourners had walked the two short miles from Jerusalem to Bethany that the sisters' living room was packed, and only Jesus was noticeable by his absence. As the hours ticked by, the women's grief must have been fraught with frustration and even resentment. They knew Jesus could have saved their brother; why didn't he come?

How often have I sent word to Jesus only to be met with a resounding silence?

I just love Martha. She gets a raw deal for being busy while her sister Mary sat at Jesus's feet, but here she teaches us what it looks like to walk Brené Brown's "collection of choices" into vulnerability and reap its rewards.

First, Go Straight to Jesus

I wish I could tell you I go straight to Jesus without a moment's hesitation when something hard happens, but more often than not I run to Google, moan to a friend, or rummage in the pantry for the last chocolate chip cookie. Finally, when I've run out of options (and cookies), I remember Jesus. But Martha doesn't hesitate. Her action-oriented nature sends her running into the village, straight to Jesus. She doesn't care about social traditions telling her it isn't the done thing. She isn't distracted by anyone or anything, not even sugary carbs.

In full view of everyone she gives him a piece of her mind: "If you had been here, my brother would not have died" (John 11:21). Her brother is dead and Jesus could have saved him.

How I've felt her grief and anger. "If you had been here, my sister wouldn't have died."

Martha knew Jesus loved her unconditionally just as he loved her brother and sister (John 11:5), and knowing this love gave her the courage and permission she needed to share her grief and frustration with him without fear of rejection.

It's never easy to leave the familiarity of my current pain and the safety of my honed-and-toned coping mechanisms to head for Jesus, but I must. It's his full life I'm desperate to breathe in, and I won't find it anywhere else—even in the last cookie or hiding in dry, snarky, passive-aggressive comments.

The only way to breathe again is to go straight to the One who is the breath of life and who breathed his life into us.

Martha knew this. She was one smart woman.

Then Turn On the Light

When we walk in vulnerability, we feel as safe as a balloon at a hedgehog party in the dark. It's terribly tempting to get the heck out of there before the fragile belief that we're loved goes pop. Our friend Martha didn't run, she just turned on the light. Truth about God always shines light into our darkness.

"Lord . . . if you had been here my brother would not have died. *But I know that even now God will give you whatever you ask*" (John 11:21–22, emphasis added).

And again, before Lazarus walks out of the tomb wrapped in bandages like a Scooby-Doo mummy, she affirms, "Yes, Lord . . . I believe that you are the Messiah, the Son of God, who is to come into the world" (John 11:27).

That's God's truth lighting the way, leading her to safety.

Can we say the same from the midst of the fog around us? "Even now, even in the midst of all my grief, I know who you are and all you can do. I trust you. You are my Savior."

What if we could?

With conflicting emotions vying for space and attention, Martha shares her darkest pain and then turns on the light of the truth. It's as if she throws it all out into the wind before landing a stake in the ground to steady herself. She knows chasing the vulnerability of our lament with truth about God grounds us, steadies the shifting sand beneath our feet, lights the way ahead, and prevents us from heading down the rabbit hole of self-pity.

As a faithful Jewish woman, she prayed like the psalmists before her: first with her heart, then her head. It must have felt familiar and comforting in the midst of her grief, and I've found this heart-to-head format transforming in my own prayers. I pour out my woes, anger, and questions to God without holding anything back, then I return to the truth of his sovereignty and love. When we pray like this, we step into the dim light of vulnerability and illuminate it with truth.

Telling your husband you're worried about your marriage and want to get help is easier when it's lit by the truth that you're deeply loved by God and your identity is in him. Turning up to a baby shower days after you've miscarried is easier lit by the truth that Jesus walks in right beside you. Telling a friend you've lost your dream job is less daunting when you're tethered to the truth that life might seem against you but God never is.

Choose Honesty over Eloquence

I can still hear my mum's words: "You're tired, it's late, it's past your bedtime, and you're beginning to show off."

As her over-bouncy third child, I constantly went to ridiculous lengths to be seen and heard amongst the family chaos, even retelling jokes everyone had only just laughed at minutes before. Over forty years later, that younger me is still alive and well and constantly fears she'll go unheard or be misunderstood. Even now as I sit at my desk I'm worried

I'll fail to articulate what I so desperately want to tell you and you'll misunderstand and miss out on God's abundance.

What if being vulnerable didn't have to be pretty or eloquent, just honest? What if we could bumble along with imperfect words, secure in who we are in Jesus? I used to think I had to have all my emotions figured out before I could begin to share them or even let people see their ugliness. If I was scared, I thought I had to know why. If I was worried, I assumed I needed a handle on what fueled the anxiety. And if my stomach lurched and my blood boiled but I had no idea what it meant, then I definitely had to keep quiet. Slowly I'm learning to just start as best I can, not waiting for perfectly crafted sentences, the whys or the wherefores, or the ideal time and place (I'm not sure they exist anyway). Simple honesty seems to be the way: "I'm scared." "I need a hug." "Why did you do that?" "I feel uncomfortable." "That makes me want to punch someone." "I can't believe this is happening." "You weren't there. I needed you."

I'm learning to share from the uncomfortable place of my unanswered questions and the messy reality of my unresolved emotions. I won't win a gold medal in debate or poetry, and I'll never be a therapist, but the prize we're after lives in our relationship with God and others, not in a trophy cupboard.

It's not eloquent, it's not fun, but it's life-giving.

I think Martha would be proud—her words weren't polished but they were honest and true to who she was, what she was feeling, and what she believed.

Knowing we are loved doesn't stop us from feeling "all the feels," but it does remove the shame and unworthiness that block us from walking in vulnerability, however clunkily, and it provides a safe place for our emotions to land. I'm learning that suppressed emotions control us, while expressed emotions heal and free us; and love cushions our vulnerability, ensuring we won't break as we venture in, giving it a go as best we can.

And You Will Find Freedom

I remember the first few times Ali showed up at church. She would slip in and out before anyone noticed, and despite desperately wanting community, she refused every invitation. She just couldn't do it. Like a bird with a broken wing, she would limp away from anyone who came close, including God.

A few months before I met Ali, while she was on a training program with work, she'd been grabbed from behind, forced into a car, and physically assaulted. Still a self-confessed emotional basket case, she moved to Charlotte and found CityChurch.

Eventually, at an evening service where Al had led us in an exercise in hearing God's voice, she took her first tentative step toward him by allowing herself to be prayed for.

Mascara dripped to the carpet from her tear-stained face as she sobbed and shook, reliving the assault, crying out to God in her pain. Slowly, she allowed herself to be scooped into the arms of a few caring souls she'd begun to trust. Ali was already in counseling twice a week, but we encouraged her to keep coming to church and keep pressing into the healing God was doing in her. Despite her circumstances, she did just that— she longed to feel better, stop hurting, and find freedom from the grip of pain and shame. Knowing something had to give eventually, she kept showing up and opening up.

Desperate to feel safe and loved, Ali walked through deep vulnerability toward God and healing and discovered how much he loves her. Finally she began to understand what his love looks and feels like. She started to believe his still small voice when it whispered, "I love you and I'm going to show you how much," and she started to imagine a life not ruled by the assault. She fell in love and got engaged.

Then came the flashback.

In a vivid visual replay of the memory her brain had suppressed, she relived the full terrifying story of what actually happened that night. Once again tears dripped to the floor as she saw herself not only physically assaulted but raped. Once again her world shattered and the girl with the broken wing limped away.

For days she just sat on her couch, staring at the floor, unable to process, suffocating under the weight of this new revelation. When she finally told me, I took her in my arms, held her, and waited for her sobbing to die down. The thought of telling her fiancé crushed her. What would he think? Would he still want her? Could he still love her? I knew hiding what happened and how she felt wouldn't protect them or their marriage, so I urged her to tell him, confident he'd react with love and compassion.

Of course he was heartbroken, but not for himself—for her. As he wrapped Ali in his arms and assured her it didn't change anything, the truth she'd vulnerably expressed in anxious trepidation set her free from the weight of her fear.

Over the next weeks she spent hours sitting in her closet, running to Jesus, drawing and journaling, pouring out her anger and pain to God, curled up on the foundation of love he'd already laid down.

There the shame of rape began to truly heal as she discovered God's grace—his crazy, wild love for her untainted by what she endured, but evident in what he endured for her. She stopped worrying she was unworthy, because two thousand years ago Jesus proved she was worthy.

Today Ali is happily married and a joy to be around. Although memories of the rape occasionally still haunt her, she says sharing her true self with God, her husband, and others heals her a little more each day and even helps others experience their own freedom.

"If you had been here, my sister wouldn't have died."

Every now and then I still feel resentment bubble up as I wonder why Jesus didn't save Mum or Jo. But I'm learning to take my cue from Martha and head down the street to meet Jesus head-on, lay it out in all its bitter ugliness and hurt questioning, and try my darnedest to follow that with what I know to be true about him.

It's not pretty, but it *is* honest, and as I confront him, this is what he says: "Oh, but I was there. I held her hand as the IV pumped chemo. I whispered peace as she tossed anxiously at night. I answered her questions as she searched for me in her darkness. And I welcomed her home as you watched her leave. I am the resurrection and the life; she believed in me and lives, even though she died."

Finding his firm foundation, I can breathe again.

Even when Jesus doesn't heal our loved ones, set us free from depression, or mend our broken marriages, let's bravely choose to walk vulnerably with God and our community to find freedom and life right where we are.

———

I am a Thriver.

I believe life doesn't have to be pain-free to be full.

I reject the lies of the world about who and whose I
am.

I embrace the truth that I am loved, seen, and enough,
and that God loves me, isn't mad, and will never
leave.

I've got this because God's got me, and together we
can do more than I could ever do alone.

I choose brave, knowing it doesn't need to be big, just
intentional.

I trust God, even when I don't want to and can't sense
his presence, because I've checked his credentials
and can let go of everything I've been clinging to.

I lean into community because thriving is a team sport
and no one wins alone.

**I step into vulnerable spaces with God and others,
aware that my strength can be my biggest
weakness.**

LEARNING TO BREATHE AGAIN

Paul says he gladly boasts in his weakness (2 Cor. 12:9). How
comfortable are you in sharing your weaknesses and fears
with others? Why might that be?

Do you find it easier to be vulnerable with God or your friends? Why do you think that is?

Read Psalm 13, noticing how verses 1–4 are a vulnerable outpouring of emotion to God while verses 5–6 follow with truth about God. Write your own psalm in this way and take time to pray it back to God. Remember, it doesn't have to be eloquent, just honest.

Is there someone you're keeping at arm's length, afraid of letting them into your pain? Could you share your feelings with them this week?

Make a note on your calendar to come back to this page next week once you've walked in vulnerability a few times. How did it go? What did it feel like? Have you started to see freedom in that area or with that person?

———◼———

Oh Jesus, it hurts. I'm confused, overwhelmed, and worried, and I don't like feeling like this. Pain is just so . . . painful and confusing.

When everything inside me wants to hide my emotions, numb them, or put them in a box labeled "Private—Keep Out," give me the courage to share them with you and with others, knowing you are safe and love me anyway. You go with me as I walk vulnerably through life, and the truth of who you are lights the way. For that I'm grateful.

Thank you for being a safe place to land when I'm drowning in emotions and can hardly breathe. Help me step into your arms with vulnerability and discover your freedom. Oh, and some joy and laughter would be nice too, please!

In your name, the name that never hides the depths of its feeling. Amen.

—— 8 ——

Embrace the Journey

Even the detours, diversions, and dead ends

Uh-oh! Mud!
Thick oozy mud.
We can't go over it.
We can't go under it.
Oh no! We've got to go through it!
Squelch squerch!
Squelch squerch!
Squelch squerch!

We're Going on a Bear Hunt

There is a time for everything,
and a season for every activity under the
     heavens: . . .
a time to weep and a time to laugh,
a time to mourn and a time to dance.

Ecclesiastes 3:1, 4

Breaking the surface of the waves, I gasped for air, my lungs burning. Before I could take a breath, another wave crashed, dragging me under, tossing me around like a pair of undies in the spin cycle. I'm a strong swimmer, but I was no match for the riptide sweeping me out to sea. I fought to get back to the beach but couldn't.

We'd stuck to the rules: swim between the two red safety flags right under the nose of the *Baywatch*-esque lifeguard who perched above the sand on what looked like an over-sized high chair, clutching his red buoy and scanning the waves. Terrifyingly quickly we were way out beyond the surfers, our towels mere specks on the distant beach. I focused on the lifeguard stand and kicked hard against the rip, but eventually I waved my arms, frantically signaling for help. We weren't getting closer to the beach; we were being dragged farther out to sea. Each time a towering breaker tumbled me, I kicked for the surface, hardly able to take a breath before the next one broke. I didn't think I could hold on much longer, and it dawned on me that I might not make it.

Unfortunately, playing by the rules doesn't mean life won't sweep us out to sea and threaten to drown us, and no amount of fighting the tide will take us back to the safety of where we started.

My cancer riptide swept me out far beyond anywhere I'd been before. Way out of my depth, fighting to breathe, terrified I wouldn't survive, I fought with every ounce of strength to swim back to shore. I just wanted to make it back, for it all to stop and go away.

Who hasn't fought against their pain and grief, desperate to return to life as it used to be? Maybe you've tossed and turned at night, wishing you could go back to the days before you knew about your husband's affair, your mother's Alzheimer's, or the rejection letter from the adoption agency. We fight emotions by burying them, we swim against the truth by welcoming the anesthesia of denial, and we cope. If we can't get back to shore, we try treading water until it's over. Isn't that better?

Eventually a young woman on her surfboard rescued me, and once safely back on the beach, I learned my mistake: I had fought against the rip. It's counterintuitive, but if you swim with the current, parallel to the shore, eventually it will bring you back to dry land. Ironically, had I known what to do, the same riptide that took me out and nearly drowned me would also have been my ticket back to the beach. Not the same stretch of beach where my towel lay waiting, but farther down and further along—a new and equally beautiful place.

What if we didn't fight the suffocating tide of our broken relationships, financial pressures, and family dysfunction, but embraced them and what God is doing in us through them, allowing him to carry our exhausted, anxious bodies somewhere new? We may not have been this way before, but he knows where we are going (Josh. 3:4).

Joy in the Journey

Rather than being dragged under by a sudden devastating diagnosis or the loss of someone close to her, Joy found herself being swept out to sea slowly, one day and one bag of cookies at a time. Her fears of getting older and remaining single mixed with the insecurities she'd carried since childhood, and she found comfort and certainty in food. Over time it became a compulsion.

The weight she gained was one thing, but the shame, unhappiness, self-loathing, and sense of being trapped weighed far more. Over a coffee and a large cinnamon bagel that sat enticingly in front of her, Joy shared with me how she continues to find healing for the damaged thinking responsible for her disordered eating: she embraces her journey with food by leaning into the daily choices set before her.

As we hugged and said our goodbyes, I noticed her half-eaten bagel still sitting there. I was brought up to clean my plate at every meal, and being full is rarely enough reason for me to leave a perfectly delicious bagel half eaten. But not Joy. As she embraces the bumpy road to freedom, she's learned to listen to her body rather than her emotions. Does she still open the fridge when she's upset or bored? Of course. She's not Superwoman. But she leans in—to her emotions, not the fridge—and listens for the lies they're whispering. Then she goes for a walk, recites God's promises, or squirts dish soap on her daughters' leftover mac and cheese, all in an act of defiance and truth, and that's where she finds joy in her freedom.

We Must Grieve to Grow

When our kids were little we loved the book *We're Going on a Bear Hunt* by Michael Rosen and Helen Oxenbury.[1] In verses that repeat the same playful, cheery refrain, it's the humorous story of a family much like ours on an adventure to find a bear. Along the way they encounter all sorts of obstacles, and with each one we would join the chorus, shouting, "We can't go over it. We can't go under it. Oh no! We've got to go through it!" before acting out squelching through the oozy mud or stumbling and tripping through the forest. Once we found the bear, we'd turn and run back through the cave, the storm, the forest, the mud, and the river before collapsing in a heap of giggles.

This simple yet profound story whispers a truth we'd rather ignore when life sweeps us out to sea. Yet, no matter how much we stick our fingers in our ears and scream, "La la la la la! I can't hear you!" this truth remains: we can't go over it, we can't go under it, we have to go through it. There's no quick fix. No getting around it.

So we might as well embrace it.

As we stop fighting the often-terrifying waves of our broken life and instead lean into them, we uncover unexpected beauty, joy, and richness we may never have discovered otherwise.

When we do the hard work of grieving, forgiving, or just admitting that life stinks right now, there will be moments of peace where there was once only anguish, flashes of hope in the darkness, and joy snuggling in with our pain as our wounds begin to heal. Embracing the journey is a gift—to you, from you, with love—because it's there we meet God.

We have to grieve to grow and move forward. Allowing ourselves to experience the breadth of our painful emotions is the only way through them and on to the waiting healing. As our friend and pastor, John, said in the days after we lost Al's mum unexpectedly, "The only way to screw up the grieving process is to not grieve."

Not long after my surgery, as I wrestled with the practical and emotional struggles of having an ostomy bag with the willfulness of a small child, we were given a week at a cabin in the heart of West Virginia. I sat on the porch, breathing in the mountain air, healing physically but not so much emotionally. I watched the kids swim, bike, and build forest forts with the boundless energy of puppies, resentful I couldn't join in. I wanted to stop the world and get off. I didn't want to be sick, I hated being an invalid, and I wished more than anything to be me—the fit, healthy mum who was game for anything and could hold her own in capture the flag.

One afternoon we tried renting two extra bikes in addition to the three we'd crammed on the back of our SUV. All five of us wanted to ride the Greenbrier River Trail, an old railroad converted to a bike path that winds peacefully beside the river. It was to be the perfect gentle day out as I gathered my strength. Unfortunately, being in the middle of nowhere, we failed miserably to find any extra bikes. So Sophie and I dropped Al, James, and Emma at the trail and drove a couple miles farther on to meet them for a picnic lunch.

We parked the car in the agreed spot and let Chester escape the confines of the boot before heading along the path, expecting to see the others any minute. It was hot—too hot for my English, medically induced menopausal internal thermostat. The mosquitoes were relentless kamikaze pilots, and my bag rumbled, threatening an explosion at any moment. It wasn't the most relaxing river walk I've been on.

The hot, sticky bikers finally appeared and devoured their sandwiches before leaping from the branch of a tree hanging invitingly over a deep pool. Chester ran up and down the bank barking, desperately trying to herd his people as they jumped and splashed before finally giving up and launching in after them. I sat alone on the picnic bench feeling sorry for myself.

Soaking up the laughter and joy, grieving my old life, the old me, and all I'd lost and could still potentially lose, I let the grief in without a fight. I felt it arrive and then, to my surprise, it slowly began to move on like the flow of the river in front of me. I felt a little bit lighter. I looked up and decided I didn't want to miss this moment. Leaving the remains of my grief and resentment at the table, I picked up my phone and started snapping shots of swimsuit-clad kids leaping for joy and one very happy, soggy dog in the midst of it all. Their shouts of delight were infectious, and although I couldn't join them in the river, I could join the fun. It didn't look like I had imagined or hoped, but it was still wonderful.

Did I deal with every last ounce of my grief and resentment that day, leaving it behind to be ravaged by mosquitos? No, but I certainly walked away lighter and fuller. I'd let some of it fall away and other parts of it heal a little, and as I did, leaning into the sucky stuff I never asked for, I discovered chief photographer and cheerleader aren't such bad roles after all.

If we are to breathe again in the midst of our mess, however imperfectly, we mustn't circumvent the healing process, no matter how much we'd like to. When we live with the pain of an unfair story, we grieve the lack of a happy ending. Yet if we rush to the end, our lives and our healing aren't nearly as rich as God intends. By the Greenbrier River I learned we must grieve to grow, and grieving the loss of our could-have-beens always helps us breathe.

Show Up

When my world is all hunky-dory and sweetness and roses, I'm more than happy to embrace the journey. But when life's fragile and uncertainty slaps me around the face, I'd rather not, thanks all the same.

Embracing the journey means getting up close and personal with our pain, and that's the last thing we want to do when life's already as fun as a root canal. When we're tired and exhausted from fighting a battle we didn't start, leaning into all those dark, threatening emotions and saying yes to unwelcome changes in our lives sounds like torture. As you know, I'd rather get a bikini wax than hang out in a room full of feelings. And despite normally loving change, I'm not quick to accept the tough, uninvited consequences of hard seasons.

Just as I should have embraced the riptide's strength and direction, finding healing and life requires us to swim with the current of our emotions. As hard as it is, we must wade through the squelchy mud and wide river, or tiptoe gently and patiently through the long dark cave, because only then will we discover the beauty buried in the poop pile.

Susan David has dedicated her life's work to the topic of emotional agility, the concept of being flexible with our thoughts and emotions. To help us respond well to situations, she encourages us to show up to them, investigating what they show us without needing to be driven by them. In my humble opinion, her TED talk should be compulsory viewing for anyone with a pulse.[2] What if we do what she suggests: notice our thoughts and feelings, name them accurately without labeling them "good" or "bad," and ask what they are telling us and what action will take us toward our values and purpose?

Is it possible to see grief as neutral—neither good nor bad in itself? Can we acknowledge that grief feels bad but isn't *inherently* bad, merely a signpost to our next step on the journey? If we can, won't that help us own and embrace the very emotions we are shying away from?

What if we show up to all our emotions? What if we own them, experiencing their depths and heights in all their Technicolor variety—refusing to label them as positive or negative—and instead use them to listen for God's next step and healing voice? If we were having a cup of tea together now, I'd whisper Susan's words into your fragile heart: "Courage is not an absence of fear; courage is fear walking."[3] And as we fear-walk through our journey, we begin to breathe again.

Will you choose brave and trust God with me so we can fear-walk hand in hand with him? Will you embrace the journey, owning all its emotions, letting them be signposts to point out his abundance along the way?

Friend, as we fear-walk with God, he says, "Do not fear for I am with you. I will never leave you or forsake you. I will be with you to the very end of the age."[4] And then, with the warm, safe, caramel-coated voice of Aslan, he calls, "Come further up, come further in."[5]

Give Yourself Permission

Although emotions may not be good or bad in and of themselves, they can still make the here and now a tough place to live. I often find myself setting up camp in the past or booking tickets for the future because it feels safer or easier than facing the yucky stuff of today.

When life's no picnic but we have warm, safe memories of our past and the future holds the promise of freedom from our current pain, it's no wonder we'd rather not deal with today.

I'm no quantum physicist, but I do know the physics of time itself mandates our presence in every single moment of every single day. Ask me what time it is and the answer will always be the same: now. Yet despite the limitations of the laws of relativity, many of us avoid or numb our "nows," not wanting to feel their broken places, but in doing so we cheat our todays of God's fullness and healing.

Unfortunately, when I hear talk of "living in the present" and being "mindful in the moment," my cheesy New Age kumbaya detector sounds the alarm. My hackles rise in anticipation of overly fluffy rhetoric that promises "you can heal your life by noticing the butterflies and the tingle of the earth beneath your toes." However, it's not all waffly nonsense.

I've never met someone more fully engaged in the present or alive to their now than Jesus. He wept, got angry and frustrated, and loved deeply. God's very name, "I Am," tells us he's the God of right now and invites us to be with him this very moment. He didn't call himself "I Might Be" (sometime in the future) or "I Used to Be" (a long time ago). His name is *I Am* (today, here, now, this very second).

Jesus forgives and heals our past and gives us hope for our future, but the empty tomb also means it's not just pie in the sky when we die, but cake on our plate while we wait! He set us free to live fully in the present, to find his abundant life today. Now.

When our world crumbles it's easy to forget how to giggle, or to wonder at life's small precious moments, or to enjoy a luxurious bubble bath and a good book. It can feel inappropriate in our current circumstances, or we simply don't have the energy. Yesterday's pain, today's stress, and tomorrow's anxiety swamp us, leaving us unable to climb out of our thick oozy mud to giggle with the kids, breathe in the beauty of the sunset, or (God forbid) enjoy a large glass of Pinot Grigio.

I figured this out at the end of a chemo "off week" when I was relatively free from the side effects of treatment. Remarkably, I didn't want to throw up or hide under my duvet feeling sorry for myself, so we bravely invited a couple of friends over for a drink on the porch. The fresh spring evening mingled with good conversation and a rare sip of wine.

But I couldn't fully relax. The relief at finally feeling human again sparred with the guilt of enjoying the company of friends. Shouldn't I be catching up on emails, doing the laundry, or more importantly, playing a board game with the kids? Was I being selfish?

The dog's bark announced the arrival of my friend Noelle with dinner for our family. I panicked: *If I'm well enough to enjoy a glass of wine and catch up with friends, surely I'm well enough to make dinner? She shouldn't have to make it for us! She mustn't see me relaxing on the porch when she's slaved over a hot stove! I'm meant to be recovering from chemo, not sipping vino.*

I needn't have worried. Noelle is grace itself, and her delight that I was well enough to enjoy a relaxed evening with no dinner preparation gave me permission to sit back and breathe in the moment. It allowed me to leave the past behind and the future with God. Grateful to be alive, I realized something profound happens when we live in the present, and with the cool porch floor tingling under my toes, I tasted some of the abundance Jesus has for me just as a butterfly fluttered by.

Where we are right now is often both the last place we want to be *and* the very place we need to be to uncover his fullness in our lives. By giving ourselves permission to live in the present, we grab hold of life in all its (pain)fullness and refuse to let go.

Travel with God

We may be surrounded by people who love us—safe people to share our deepest fears with—but at the end of the day, suffering is a lonely place. You're the only one who sleeps next to that empty pillow each night after losing your husband. You're the only one who battles with your anxiety or wrestles with your looming fear of never conceiving.

Every time I read the book of Ruth, I'm gobsmacked by Ruth's decision to stick with Naomi. Surely she'd already endured enough? Why on earth would she leave her homeland in the midst of her grief, parting from her extended family and the safety of all she knew, to head off with her mother-in-law to a place and people she didn't know?

I love my mother-in-law, but if we were still living in England and Al's father died, leaving her a widow, and then Al and his two brothers kicked the bucket as well, I'm not convinced I'd be so quick to follow if she decided to return to her homeland—a place I'd never been. No ma'am. I'd be with Orpah, Ruth's sister-in-law, plonking a quick peck on Naomi's cheek before staying put. She had Naomi's blessing after all, and grief persuades us to cling to what we know, not embrace the unknown road ahead.

Ruth must have felt the waves of grief sweep her out to sea, the loneliness of widowhood crash in on her, and the fear of the famine sweeping the land take her breath every time she came up for air. But she didn't fight. She leaned into the hunger pangs, the social pressure to stay with her people, and the ticking clock inside her belly telling her to seek another husband. She let them guide her like road signs from God. She turned and clung to Naomi and Naomi's God, who she'd made her own. She swam parallel to the shore of her grief and let the tide take her to solid ground where she found life and a husband.

God met Ruth on her journey and he will meet us on ours too. It's only with him that we can breathe his life and fullness as we journey on. Ruth couldn't run from the loss of her husband, but she could have run from Naomi's invitation to a new land. The trouble was, through her husband's family and faith Ruth had discovered the one true God and the life he gives. Could she turn away now? She'd rather head into the unknown with God than back to the familiar without him.

I wanted to run from my cancer like Usain Bolt sprinting for Olympic gold, not embrace it or sit around long enough to learn what it was teaching me. I didn't want to look for the beauty in the ashes; I just wanted to sweep the ashes away. I wanted my cancer to get cancer and die because I liked the beauty of my old life, thanks all the same. I wanted to stand and fight, be strong, then lie down and go to sleep.

People often say life's a journey, but this girl never bought a ticket—someone must have drugged me, tied me in a mail sack, and thrown me on the cancer train. But I was on that train whether I liked it or not, and there was no emergency brake. I could go with it or fight it. I could go with God or fly solo. Either way the train had left the station.

God is here in the midst of our pitiful todays, and when we fight the journey we fight against him and reject his goodness. By traveling on with God, accepting what we cannot change, leaning into our emotions, reading them like signposts in a desert, we land in an oasis of freedom and hope rather than a dry, dusty wasteland of bitterness and resentment. And nothing thrives in the desert outside an oasis.

I am a Thriver.

I believe life doesn't have to be pain-free to be full.

I reject the lies of the world about who and whose I am.

I embrace the truth that I am loved, seen, and enough, and that God loves me, isn't mad, and will never leave.

I've got this because God's got me, and together we can do more than I could ever do alone.

I choose brave, knowing it doesn't need to be big, just intentional.

I trust God, even when I don't want to and can't sense his presence, because I've checked his credentials and can let go of everything I've been clinging to.

I lean into community because thriving is a team sport and no one wins alone.

I step into vulnerable spaces with God and others, aware that my strength can be my biggest weakness.

I embrace the good, the bad, and the ugly of my journey, knowing the only way out is through and there's life and healing to be found along the way.

LEARNING TO BREATHE AGAIN

Here are some suggestions for leaning in and processing what you're going through. Choose one that fits who you are and commit to leaning into it this week.

Journaling. Writing our emotions helps us put shape and form to often hidden feelings and gives us the language to vulnerably share them with others.

Counseling. Taking time to talk things through with a professional who is trained to help us deal with our stuff helps us uncover and process emotions we don't know how to navigate ourselves.

Me Time. Whether time with friends, a bubble bath, a day at the spa, or sitting with a cup of tea and a good book, time invested in ourselves is more than compensated by the healing and space it gives our weary souls.

Letter Writing. Penning a letter you'll never post to someone you've lost, someone who's hurt you, or to God, letting all your feelings flow out untethered, helps us figure out what we're feeling.

Support Group. Finding a safe, supportive group that talks about what you're dealing with—such as AA, grief groups, or cancer support groups—is a great way to process our emotions in the safety of others who've been where we are.

As you process and emotions bubble to the surface, try not to judge them, dismiss them, or negate them. They are your emotions and they are real and valid.

Try naming five emotions (difficult or not) you've felt in the last week. How might they be signposts to the next step in your journey?

How might you give yourself permission to live in your "now" moments? What might that look like practically?

Have you been excluding or including God in your journey? What would it look like to invite him in as you navigate this season?

———

Oh Lord, I'm so grateful Jesus wasn't just a man of the moment but a man in the moment. Help me be the same and embrace this journey I've found myself on.

When I'm swept out to sea on a riptide of emotions, help me grieve and grow, owning them even when they scare me. They are real, they are mine, and I am yours, so all will be well.

Thank you, Lord, for walking hand in hand with me on this journey and being the best traveling companion I could ever ask for. Help me see the beauty in the ashes along the way, and show me it's okay to laugh and feel the grass between my toes.

In the name of your Son, Jesus, who is with me right this minute and will be always. Amen.

9

Practice Gratitude

For the rubble, not just the rubies

It's only with gratitude that life becomes rich.

Dietrich Bonhoeffer

Rejoice always, pray continually, give thanks in all circumstances; for this is God's will for you in Christ Jesus.

1 Thessalonians 5:16–18

Our first Thanksgiving in America was a joke. As Brits we had absolutely no idea what to do. It was pitiful. Should we go away or stay home? What about turkey? Good grief, no. If you're from my side of the pond, turkey is for Christmas, and I didn't want to wrestle a big bird twice in two months. All our new friends were with their families, so we were flying solo on this one, and without a road map carved from years of family traditions, we were lost. What should we do? What should we eat? What on earth is sweet potato pie? And would someone, for the love of the game, please explain a third down and why they don't pass backwards like they do in rugby back home?

Our kids had learned the story of the first Thanksgiving at school, and we could see what a beautiful time of gratitude and family gathering it was to our friends, so in the end we rented a cabin in the mountains and I bought an oversized chicken potpie from Costco. I know, not exactly your traditional Thanksgiving fare. But we'd had a crazy year: three moves (one internationally), three kids in two new schools (where they were constantly asked to "say something British" or "speak like Harry Potter"), along with the birthing pains of planting CityChurch and the ache of leaving home. We needed a break.

We also needed a bit of refocusing.

Giving thanks would be a good thing. The last year had been exhausting and at times painful, but we still had much to be grateful for. Wherever we looked we could see God's goodness, but we were long overdue with our gratitude.

We headed to the North Carolina mountains to begin our own Thanksgiving traditions of talent shows, chicken potpie, long hikes, playing sardines in the dark, and lazy days. We gave thanks for the good and ignored the rest.

Thanksgiving: A Holiday or a Lifestyle?

Ignored the rest. Did I really type that? Oh dear. The Bible tells us over eighty times to be "grateful," "give thanks," or do things "with thanksgiving." Psychologists tell us gratitude increases not just our well-being but also our happiness, optimism, connection, and empathy, and it reduces aggression.[1] If being grateful is so darn good for me, why don't I live in a constant state of gratitude? Why do I struggle to give thanks at all? Perhaps (and I'm ashamed to say this) because when things are good I get caught up in life and forget to give thanks, and when things are bad I get sucked into the suckiness of it all and it's hard to see anything worthy of my thanks. (Worthy? Really? Did I type that as well?)

All those benefits of gratitude that psychologists have discovered—empathy, connection, optimism (hope), and happiness—aren't they what God's abundant, full life looks like? If that's true (and I think it is), then if we want to breathe him in, we must somehow learn to be grateful whether our days are bright and breezy or darkened by storm clouds. We can't wait until the pages of our lives reflect the happily ever after we've ordered. We can't look down our noses at the lives we're living, only deigning to give thanks when something's worthy of our approval.

I'll admit, as I struggled with cancer and dealt with my anger and grief from losing Mum and Jo, my underwhelmed faith and overwhelmed heart were as predisposed to thanksgiving as a teenager is to spontaneously tidying their room. Despite being commanded to give thanks, and in spite of the tangible benefits of doing so, I looked around me and saw a father who'd lost his daughter, two sisters where once there were three, children afraid their mum might die, a strong man of faith challenged by his wife's suffering, and a bag of poop on my belly where my children once snuggled. It wasn't always easy to see anything worth bursting into spontaneous

147

cries of gratitude for. It's as if cancer had given me polarized glasses filtering out any beauty and light.

Being grateful in every situation—good, bad, or ugly—requires a gratitude mind-set, not just grateful moments. If we can turn gratitude from an individual thought into a way of thinking, giving thanks in all things at all times, we can live a full life and not just full moments.

The Give Thanks in All Things Game

I think my next book might be titled *Flying with Small Children: A Survival Guide for Mums*. You name it, we've done it: delays, cancellations, rerouting in midair, terrifying turbulence, lost luggage, nights on airport chairs, overflowing motion sickness bags, and angry fellow passengers. Been there, done that, and got the air miles to prove it.

After one particularly bad flight, while we waited at the back of a never-ending "re-ticketing because your delayed flight has now been canceled completely" line, we invented the Give Thanks in All Things Game. Less about true gratitude and more about stopping the kids' moaning, we explained the aim of the game in overly chirpy "let's prevent meltdown" voices: *God tells us to give thanks in all things, including flight delays and I-want-to-go-home moments, so let's see how many things we find to be thankful for and say why we're grateful.* Escalators made the top of the list (for their leg-saving genius), followed by the sweet lady who lent Sophie her pillow to sleep on the floor (sleep is always a good thing). But also making the list were the canceled flight itself (seeing people be kind when life isn't) and being at the back of the queue (time to grab a Starbucks snack).

It worked. The whining stopped. To this day we still play the Give Thanks in All Things Game, and we're working on making it a way of life, not just a game in life.

When doctors sliced me open, rerouted my God-given plumbing, and left me wondering if this was it, I tried to play the game despite my feelings. Once again it was less about gratitude and more about trying to exchange my whining for God's whispers. I knew he commands us to give thanks and to do it in *all* circumstances, even in the stench of a leaking ostomy bag, so I tried. I looked around and started naming things I was grateful for.

Top of my list was "not dying." A bit melodramatic, I know, but it wasn't guaranteed and I was grateful to still be breathing. But apart from that, I struggled. True, I hadn't popped my clogs, Al hadn't run off with my disarmingly stunning nurse, and my kids weren't snorting cocaine behind the bleachers (yet), but I didn't feel grateful. I was mid-chemo for a tumor in an unmentionable orifice, I'd just lost my big sister to cancer in the ugliest of battles, I worried my bag of poop would pop if I was hugged too tight, nausea and neuropathy followed me around like boy-band groupies, and my kids had to live with the fear their mum might be sipping tea in heaven's tea shop sometime soon. What was there to be grateful for?

Then I remembered Corrie ten Boom's story. She and her sister Betsie were imprisoned in a concentration camp during World War II for their role in the Dutch Resistance. Crammed into barracks, hungry, freezing, exhausted, and with her sister getting sicker by the day, Corrie agreed to "give thanks in all things" as a way to endure their time there. When Betsie, always more serene and spiritual than the impetuous

Corrie, gave thanks for the fleas biting their legs and scalps, Corrie couldn't believe it.

> "Betsie, there's no way even God can make me grateful for a flea."
>
> "'Give thanks in *all* circumstances,'" she quoted. "It doesn't say, 'in pleasant circumstances.' Fleas are part of this place where God has put us."
>
> And so we stood between piers of bunks and gave thanks for fleas. But this time I was sure Betsie was wrong.[2]

Over the weeks the women held worship services at the back of their cramped quarters and lived in fear the guards would come in and see what they were doing, but they never did. Then they found out why—the guards wouldn't enter the barracks because of the fleas. Corrie continues: "My mind rushed back to our first hour in this place. I remembered Betsie's bowed head, remembered her thanks to God for creatures I could see no use for."[3]

Just as Corrie ten Boom could see no use for the fleas, I could see no use for my cancer, and like her I didn't want to give thanks for any part of it. But I was commanded to.

"Rejoice always, pray continually, give thanks in all circumstances; for this is God's will for you in Christ Jesus" (1 Thess. 5:16–18). Always. Continually. All. I guess I didn't have a choice. Not only was it a command but it was, and is, God's will for my life. And since his will is good, pleasing, and perfect (Rom. 12:2), I had to believe somehow it was best for me. So I did, finally, bit by stubborn bit. As an act of obedience I began to give thanks for the whole lot. The poop bag, the leaks, the chemo. Even the fragility of my life.

I began to develop an attitude of gratitude by stepping into life with intention despite my circumstances. Then and only then did the gratitude needle begin to shift from, as Bekah Pogue says, holiday to lifestyle, from game to habit.[4]

A Command with a Promise

Expressing gratitude for the tough and broken as well as the shiny and whole began ever so slowly to shift my gaze. When I gave thanks for my ostomy bag, it morphed from a farting, leaking bulge on my midriff to a life-giving medical miracle allowing me to heal and poop at the same time—even while worshiping in church. The nausea became proof the chemo was fighting any cancer cells that had escaped to other parts of my body. With gratitude, the worry on my children's faces opened doors for extra hugs and deep conversations we'd never ventured into before.

Fresh life grew from those small acts of obedient thanksgiving.

The quieting of the pain that demands our attention, the bubbling up of storm-calming goodness, the refocusing from what brings us pain to what fills us up—aren't these God's promises? They're the promises Paul talked about when he told us to come to God in thanksgiving: "And the peace of God, which transcends all understanding, will guard your hearts and your minds in Christ Jesus" (Phil. 4:7).

I wanted more than anything for everything bad and painful to disappear. I wanted to pull the emergency handle on the cancer train and get off and stop feeling so crappy, but that wasn't going to happen anytime soon. I found practicing gratitude didn't lessen the pain but magnified the beauty and wrapped everything in a calming peace. I didn't stop feeling nauseous or worried, but instead my capacity to feel happy, peaceful, and optimistic grew.

Little did I know I was living proof of all that positive psychology research showing how gratefulness enhances our well-being. In her *Forbes* article, Amy Morin lists seven proven benefits of gratitude.[5] As I read them, I see God's promises from 1 Thessalonians 5:18 in the hard data: better sleep, improved physical and psychological health, increased mental strength and self-esteem. Gratitude even increases empathy and reduces aggression, which I know my family was grateful for in their chemo-induced snarky mother. Whether it's Vietnam veterans, survivors of 9/11, or regular folks going about their daily lives, research shows time and again that gratitude has a profound effect on our well-being—or as the Bible calls it, "abundance."

Often we're brought up to believe God is all about rules and regulations, barking "do," "don't," and "you'd better not or else" with the controlling harshness of a drill sergeant. We couldn't be more wrong. That's not who he is. His voice brims with love and longing. His "no" is never bellowed to control us or ruin our happiness but uttered with the pleading tenderness of a father's aching heart. *My dear sweet child, don't. You'll get hurt, which is the last thing I want for you. It would break my heart because I love you.*

What if we saw his command to give thanks not as a controlling, guilt-inducing order to fill his ego but as a loving plea from the One who knows what's best for us? *Live gratefully, my child, because when you do, all these promises are yours, and I so want you to experience all I have for you.*

We can practice a lifestyle of gratitude because God tells us to *and* because when we do he promises to pour out blessings. He turns our gratitude into goodness, adds peace to our pain, and provides strength in our struggles. God commands us not as a manipulative bully but as a loving Father whose will is good and always comes with his promise of peace.

Just ask a psychologist if you need any more proof. We don't need to see things differently to be grateful; rather, we must be grateful to see things differently. And when we do, when we see it *all* and give thanks for it *all* at *all* times, "Before you know it, a sense of God's wholeness, everything coming together for good, will come and settle you down. It's wonderful what happens when Christ displaces worry at the center of your life" (Phil. 4:7 MSG).

The Gratitude of No Ordinary Teenager

Outwardly, Mary seemed like a normal teenager—nothing to write home about. Like most girls her age, she was already betrothed and had her life mapped out in front of her: marry the carpenter Joseph, have a few kids, and live happily ever after while honoring and trusting God. She was no different from any of her girlfriends, until a tall, dark, and handsome angel made a heavenly appearance in her living room. (Okay, so there's no biblical evidence Gabriel is George Clooney with wings, but can't a girl imagine?)

Gabriel throws an almighty curveball at Mary's nice, calm, planned-out life, sending it completely off course. Before this encounter her life wasn't exactly to die for, but being chosen to be the unwed mother of the Messiah was no upgrade. She knew all too well what it meant: as an unmarried, pregnant teenager, she faced divorce and possibly death. Her good Jewish parents—along with the rest of her community—would tear their clothes, mortified, then disown and shun her. In a nutshell, Gabriel's news shattered Mary's world.

I just love Mary. On the one hand she is so human and relatable, and on the other she's a spiritual marvel—the woman I want to be when I grow up. This shattering knocks her for six, but after she questions her heavenly messenger about a few practical details and takes a moment to think, she's all in (Luke 1:26–38).

I wonder if she knew what she was getting into or if Gabriel's heavenly presence and (I imagine) piercing blue eyes worked some heavenly spell. What happened when the light faded and his heavenly glow was just a memory? Did she question it as a moment of hormonal madness? Did she panic at the thought of what could lie ahead? We'll never know.

Another mystery is why Mary hurried to her cousin Elizabeth's house. I wonder if she made the ninety-mile trek through the hill country between Nazareth and Judea feeling more and more anxious, her heart at sixes and sevens with what she'd agreed to. While it's likely she was among a caravan of travelers, she would have been alone with her thoughts and her worsening morning sickness.

We don't know what she thought as she made this journey, but we do know the first thing she did once Elizabeth greeted her: she praised God and gave thanks. This teenage unwed mother, in danger of divorce and possible death, gave thanks for her God and how he had looked with favor on her (Luke 1:46–49).

Favor? Really?

From the outside looking in, gratefully calling herself favored sounds like utter madness; but from the inside looking out it makes perfect sense. Mary knew this shattering was for her good and for the good of all people, and thanksgiving was the way to finding life within it.

Gratitude: An Action, Not a Feeling

Two months before I was diagnosed, I ran my first marathon with a few friends from church. Now, before you get too impressed, I should mention it was all downhill. A bit of a cheat, I know, but I needed all the help I could get if I was going to run 26.2 miles.

My goal was fourfold: (1) finish; (2) no tears; (3) no blood; and (4) beat Oprah (she ran the Marine Corps Marathon in 4:29:20 in 1994). I set the bar pretty low. I'm that kind of high achiever.

Training for a marathon is almost a full-time job. We ran five days a week and I'll admit, three of those I didn't even want to put my shoes on. My muscles were sore from all that pavement pounding, I was constantly tired, and I struggled to fit the long runs into my week. If it wasn't for my BRB (best running buddy) Winn, the positive physical and emotional changes I saw, and the habit I was forming, I probably would have skipped more than I did.

I ran when I didn't feel like it because I knew the promise of getting stronger and fitter was real and tangible. I ran when I least wanted to because I knew it was a discipline my body could learn. And I ran when the sofa, a family pack of peanut M&M's, and the latest episode of *Downton Abbey* were calling my name because I knew I'd feel better if I did.

What if we treated practicing gratitude in the same way we train for a marathon—in daily steps toward a greater goal? What if we stopped waiting to *feel* grateful and were grateful anyway, believing God is good and has more for us? Gratitude is nothing more than the act of giving thanks before we might feel like it. As Robert Emmons says, "It is vital to make a distinction between *feeling* grateful and *being* grateful. We don't have total control over our emotions. We cannot easily will ourselves to feel grateful, less depressed, or happy. Feelings follow from the way we look at the world, thoughts we have about the way things are, the way things should be, and the distance between these two points."[6]

My friend Kristan is a genius at this.

Flip the Script

Kristan is a ball of energy. She's a mum of five, a counselor, writer, speaker, and breast cancer survivor who teaches group exercise classes at the YMCA. Just writing about her life exhausts me—especially since she's a triple amputee.

Just after the birth of her fifth baby, Kristan assumed her fitness and flu shot were why she'd avoided all the winter bugs. But then the double whammy of strep throat on top of a bad case of the flu spiraled her into septic shock, almost killing her. Not many people make it through septic shock, but after three weeks in a medically induced coma and one hundred days in six different hospitals, a powerful treatment saved her life—but at the cost of her hands and feet.

Today, having lost both arms just below her elbows, one foot from just below her knee, and the heel and toes on her one remaining foot, she manages to smile, joking that she's lost three and a half limbs.

Of course she'd take her hands back in a heartbeat.

You bet she wishes it had never happened.

And yet she's grateful for the good that's come from this in her marriage, her children, her faith, in the people she's met along the way, and in her own outlook on life.

Speaking of being grateful in the pain seems easy for her now. She's quick to notice the way people open up to her when her prosthetics reveal her vulnerability, how the staff at her local Aldi can read her mood and know when she wants help and when it's best to leave her to do it alone, or how children ask how she lost her arms with a boldness that mortifies their parents. She's grateful for these moments.

Even when pain keeps her up at night, she thanks God he's there with her as she feels his comfort.

Ironically, Kristan was in the middle of doing a thirty-day gratefulness challenge for Thanksgiving when she got sick. She only made it to November 23, but has picked up where she left off. She now writes down three things she's grateful for each day and even gives this as homework to her therapy patients. Reminding them it takes patience, practice, and intention, she teaches them to flip their script and change "I have to" into "I get to." As she lets me in on some of her self-talk exercises, I'm inspired and challenged.

"I have to do eight loads of laundry" becomes "I get to do eight loads of laundry today because I have an automatic machine, clean hot water, and five beautiful children with more than enough clothes to wear."

"I have to drive carpool" becomes "I get to pick up my girls from soccer and hear them chatter with their friends. I get to drive when I never thought I'd get behind the wheel again, let alone turn a key in the ignition."

By flipping the script, she flips her attitude from pain to praise, groaning to gratitude.

Change one word, change your outlook. That's her motto, and she is living proof it works.

Don't get me wrong. She's not a happy-skippy, walking-talking bundle of gratefulness who never gets angry, frustrated, or overwhelmed. She may have arms with battery packs, but she's not superhuman. But she is convinced. Convinced there's more of life to be grabbed, even with prosthetic hands. Convinced her outlook can be changed by her thoughts and actions. She knows changing her outlook takes purposeful practice, and even if that practice doesn't make things perfect, it does make them easier. The more the frustration and anger fade, the more she sees the positive results of feeling more alive and the more she wants to be grateful, until finally she doesn't have to remind herself anymore.

Thanksgiving has become an outlook and a lifestyle for this featherweight fighter.

Kristan's life is far from easy. Her storm isn't going to blow over next week or even next year. She could roll over and give up, but she doesn't. Instead she chooses to flip the script and give thanks in all things, just like her hero the apostle Paul implored. Against all the odds Kristan squeezes every last drop out of the new and painful life she never signed up for.

When our pain screams, our gratitude must shout louder—not to deny it but to drown it out with praise. When we're fighting addiction, experiencing chronic pain, enduring chemo, or overwhelmed with caring for an aging parent, gratitude is hard, but it is possible. Practicing gratitude is an intentional act of faith, saying yes to God's command and will for our lives. Like so many steps of faith, it brings blessing as we plant our feet in front of us, however tentatively, remembering two steps forward and one step back is still progress.

I still struggle to run when I haven't got the energy, and I'm still learning to be grateful even when I don't feel it. I'm still learning to lean into the cracks and tears of my life and choose to thank God for them. It's not easy but it is possible, and as William Wordsworth is rumored to have said, "To begin, begin." Let's dive in, whether we feel like it or not, knowing and trusting the water we dive into is the living, life-giving water of the One whose abundance we crave.

I am a Thriver.

I believe life doesn't have to be pain-free to be full.

I reject the lies of the world about who and whose I am.

I embrace the truth that I am loved, seen, and enough, and that God loves me, isn't mad, and will never leave.

I've got this because God's got me, and together we can do more than I could ever do alone.

I choose brave, knowing it doesn't need to be big, just intentional.

I trust God, even when I don't want to and can't sense his presence, because I've checked his credentials and can let go of everything I've been clinging to.

I lean into community because thriving is a team sport and no one wins alone.

I step into vulnerable spaces with God and others, aware that my strength can be my biggest weakness.

I embrace the good, the bad, and the ugly of my journey, knowing the only way out is through and there's life and healing to be found along the way.

I practice gratitude in all things, confident that peace and well-being will follow.

LEARNING TO **BREATHE AGAIN**

Here are some ways Kristan and I practice gratitude.

- Set a time and place each day to be thankful. Five minutes before bed is a good one.
- Keep a gratitude log, naming three things to be grateful for each day.
- Write a letter to God telling him all you're grateful for and asking him to show you the good he is working in the things that seem all pain and no purpose.
- Write a list of all the people you're grateful for. Write them thank-you notes, being specific about what it is you really appreciate them for.
- Take five minutes a few times a day to breathe deeply as you visualize a few things around you that you are thankful for.

- Flip the script when you hear yourself moaning, complaining, or spiraling down. How can you turn "I have to" into "I get to"?

Which of these practices might you commit to doing on a regular basis?

Oh Lord, I'm sorry for being an ungrateful Moaning Minnie at times. It's so hard to give thanks when I can't see anything worth being grateful for. Help me see things differently.

Lord, I'm grateful for you, for your love, and for your Son. I'm thankful you're in this with me and won't ever leave me. You're showing me so much, teaching me, guiding and steering me, and for that I'm thankful.

Help me lean into gratitude as a way of life, not waiting to feel grateful but trusting that your command leads to life and fullness. Nudge me when I moan and teach me how I can flip the script to see all that is good in my life.

In the name of Jesus, the one whose life, death, and resurrection I am eternally grateful for. Amen.

=== 10 ===

Reach Out

It might just save you

We make a living by what we get, but we make a life by what we give.

Winston Churchill

Give, and it will be given to you. A good measure, pressed down, shaken together and running over, will be poured into your lap.

Luke 6:38

I was too tired and selfish to help anyone else.

Once again I'm embarrassed by my blatant self-preservation, but hey-ho, we're old friends now and I confess, I ran at the first whiff of somebody else's neediness. I could barely hold my own fractured life together, so being the glue in somebody else's shattered world was just too much.

Perhaps you feel the same. Maybe you flinched when you read this chapter title and muttered into your coffee, *You're kidding me! She wants me to do what? I'm already running on fumes. How can I help anyone else?*

I get it. You're loving yourself well, figuring out how to grab your broken and painfully beautiful life and squeeze the juice out of it, and now I'm asking you to give what little energy you have away? Pour out what's taken you so long to fill up? I know it's a bit of a bombshell, but hear me out.

Let me tell you about Vicki.

The Myth of Costly Kindness

As cancer took over my life, I felt like a shipwrecked sailor, rationing what little energy the disease hadn't stolen into people-sized portions, praying my dwindling supplies would last and I wouldn't have to eat anyone (just kidding). I carefully divided it between family and just a few close friends, always looking to replenish stocks whenever I could. You see, I'd bought into the myth of costly kindness, the belief that being there for others comes at a huge personal cost.

Then I met Vicki.

We sat in awkward silence in the women's locker room of the radiation department, our hospital gowns gapping precariously round our knees and our cancer diagnoses sitting like two large elephants (also in matching, standard-issue green hospital gowns) squeezed between us.

Whatever cancer she was battling, Vicki was clearly having a rough ride. Her pink scalp glared through wisps of what remained of her hair, and she sucked desperately on a mint as her dry, cracked lips threatened to split and bleed.

On previous visits I'd politely exchanged pleasantries with fellow patients but had never ventured beyond the safety of the weather. There'd never been time; we were marshaled off to our various treatment rooms with military precision, and anything beyond that seemed too personal, too intrusive.

But here we sat, with only her mint sucking to fill the silence. Things were running behind and a dearth of the usual waiting room glossy magazines gave us a choice: make eye contact and say hi or continue in awkward silence. Extroverts don't like silence; it makes us squirm. So I broke protocol.

Offering a dusty throat lozenge I'd scavenged from the depths of my bag, I smiled and said hello.

As I suspected, she was having a dreadful time. Mouth cancer had left her nauseous, with painful sores and a constantly parched mouth due to the destruction of her salivary glands. We chatted and shared our stories. Feeling totally helpless, I told her how sorry I was and gently laid my hand on her arm. I offered to pray; it was all I had.

Eventually I was called to get my butt zapped, so we hugged and exchanged a smile of solidarity and understanding. I never saw Vicki again, but I left our little encounter more alive than when I arrived. I learned that sharing someone's burden, even for a moment, isn't the drain we imagine but a tank-filling privilege and joy. I hadn't offered a single piece of advice or practical support—I had none to offer. I just sat with her, listened, and agreed that yes, life really does stink sometimes.

I'd been wrong. Afraid of being sucked down by the undertow from someone else's sinking life, I had secured my life vest and was focused solely on those in my lifeboat. In that waiting room I discovered that lifting someone up doesn't need to bring us down. It doesn't need to be some big all-singing, all-dancing act of chivalrous self-sacrifice that drains our precious reserves. And Jesus was right—as I gave I received and was filled up beyond the fraction I'd poured out (Luke 6:38).

Vicki showed me that when we turn our heart toward another and away from self-protection, small acts of kindness have the power to lighten their load and brighten our darkness without great cost to ourselves.

You Have Something Unique to Offer

I still don't know what I want to be when I grow up. As I write this, I'm about to turn the big five-oh, and despite writing this book I still wonder if I have anything to offer. I'm not a teacher, doctor, singer, or counselor, and I doubt whether multitasking, carpool-driving, teenage-drama-soothing, tea-drinking dog lover is really that unique. After my diagnosis I added poop-cleaning, ostomy-wearing, short-tempered cancer patient to that list of accolades and struggled even more to see anything unique I could offer the world. So I could relate to the servant of Naaman's wife.

She was a nobody, an unnamed servant to an unnamed mistress, and had been kidnapped to a strange land far from home. She served in the household of Naaman, a highly regarded army commander for the king of Aram, who struggled with the pain and social stigma of being covered in leprosy.

Scripture dedicates just two short verses to this young woman who is kinder than I'll be in a month of Sundays

(2 Kings 5:2–3). And yet we're given a glimpse not just into her world but into her heart, and we're left asking, do we really have nothing to offer?

She might have been far from home, but she carried her faith with her. Despite the grief and resentment she must have felt at being snatched from her family, she suggested to her mistress that Naaman seek healing from God through the prophet Elisha in Samaria. Desperate, Naaman jumps at the chance to be rid of his horrific sores, and after a series of events he's healed of the disease that had plagued him for so long. All thanks to the young woman he'd taken into captivity and whose name he may have never even known.

I wouldn't have blamed her if she'd kept quiet. Teenage Niki would probably have smiled smugly, knowing her God could easily heal her master but stayed silent, too resentful and hurt to help. But not this teenager. She didn't let her external hardship or internal turmoil stop her from giving the one thing she had that Naaman didn't: the source of his healing. By seeing Naaman as God saw him, her one small act of kindness—a short sentence uttered to her mistress—gave him first hope and then healing.

How many times in my pain and resentment have I withheld love or kindness? How many times have I looked at a situation and seen something too big to impact from my worn-out corner of the world where I sit feeling empty-handed and sorry for myself? How many times have I failed to see someone as God sees them and walked right by, focused on my own hurt? But our hands aren't empty, they are *full*, and God gives us eyes to see others. Even with broken hearts we can mourn with those who mourn and comfort those who need comforting because now more than ever we understand their pain. Now we can offer the gift of empathy and not just sympathy.

You have something unique and special to give that no one else can. You are important and needed even if you don't feel like it. Look around you. What do you see? What seems so simple or obvious to you might be life-changing and beautiful to someone else. That dish you cook every week, the one your kids groan about because they're sooooo bored of it? It's perfect for the young mum a couple of doors down struggling to juggle her new baby and get food on the table. I'm sure she wouldn't moan if you made it for her. You know how you love those Bible verses you have set to pop into your phone each morning? I bet if you sent one to your recently divorced hairdresser, she'd feel loved and encouraged.

I wonder, as the Christmas carols suggest, whether the shepherd who brought his lamb to baby Jesus beat himself up, thinking, "I can't believe I'm bringing this stupid sheep. You can't move in Bethlehem for sheep; they're everywhere. I wish I had something big and special to give." But it was all he had and he went anyway, despite any fear he had nothing unique to bring.

It All Adds Up

Unlike me, Al isn't fazed by mountainous tasks. Twenty thousand photos in the cloud to be sorted and put into albums? No problem. He just chips away, sorting a hundred or so a couple of times a week until lickety-split, our photos are ordered and searchable. Me? I just need to catch a glimpse of the task towering above me and I lie down and roll over, defeated.

When this book—all forty-five thousand words of it— gets published, it will be a miracle spurred on by Al's encouragement to chip away. Word by word, page by page, day by day.

The trouble is when we're tired and hurting, helping others looms over us like Everest against a sunlit sky: imposing and unscalable. But we can love others, word by word, step by step, chipping away one small act of kindness at a time. I may not be able to move a mountain, but I can pick up a pebble—and so can you, and that makes two. At the time it feels insignificant and hardly worth the effort, but I can assure you, having been on the receiving end of hundreds of small acts of love, that each encouraging text, each "hug in a casserole," and each listening ear add up. They are like a cool sip of water in the midday sun.

My friend Todd is a genius at this. Despite living with chronic pain, he seems to cultivate a chipping-away mentality to reaching out in his daily life. So much so, he actually sees his pain as a gift. A word of empathy here, a promise of hope there, a scattering of "you're not alone" left in his wake.

This isn't a man who has mild backache. Oh no. On good days he endures headaches that would send me to bed, cool cucumbers on my eyes and soothing whale songs playing in the background. On rough days he can't leave the house, and on terrible days he's hospitalized. The pain's never given him a day off, and no one can tell him where it comes from, but he says since so many people deal with chronic pain, he has a unique opportunity to journey with them one step at a time.

We Can't Out-Give the Giver Himself

Todd's seen so many doctors he's lost count, and as far as he knows his pain will never end, so he's had to dig deep to uncover the full life he knows Jesus has for him, right there in the depths of his blinding pain. Todd is certain finding that abundance is tied to his call and purpose: to love his family and encourage others in chronic pain. It's that simple.

The key, he says, is he can't out-give Jesus. Each word of support he offers a fellow sufferer, each gift of hope he shares, each encouragement he gives to others in pain, telling them they are seen and understood, changes his perspective on life. It shifts his focus from himself and his pain and confirms what he's always believed: God gave us gifts to encourage one another, we are to use them no matter how we feel, and we will always receive far more than we can ever give. Because the remarkable thing is, when Todd's encouraging others or preaching sermons, he experiences absolutely no pain.

All I'd done for Vicki was smile, say hi, listen, and utter a short, rather awkward prayer. When we parted I wasn't drained, desperate to refill my emotional and physical energy levels. Quite the opposite. I felt lighter, filled up, and I too felt seen and loved. God had been present in that one small moment, and my smile and lightness went with me into my day. Isn't that what his fullness looks like?

When Jesus sent the disciples out into the world, he finished his instructions by telling them whoever loses their life will find it, and whoever welcomes them welcomes him and therefore God (Matt. 10:39–40). What if the same is true with loving others? What if, in a miraculous upside-down exchange, we find more of life as we give it out? When we welcome others by showing them they are seen and known, aren't we welcoming Jesus? And if we welcome him, even tentatively, we welcome his Father and the full life he paid to give us. Can we give out of what little we have, confident we'll be filled up more? Can we trust God enough to give what little we have and see our lives come into focus as we welcome Jesus—the very source of the abundance we so crave?

The world is quick to tell us we'll find our purpose and live fully and abundantly when our pain is a memory and we have time and energy to spare, but that's a load of baloney. God is the master storyteller, and like every writer who's come after him, he knows the real adventure—the one where we come fully alive—happens between once upon a time and happily ever after, and it always involves our reaching out to others along the way.

How to Give When You Have Nothing to Offer

The idea of striking up a conversation with a woman you've never met while wearing nothing but a green hospital gown might be your idea of a nightmare, but never fear. There are oodles of ways to reach out and love someone without draining what little fuel reserves you have left in your tank.

I'm not the most creative bunny on the block, but here are some ways people loved me at little cost to them and that I've done for others in return.

Send an encouraging text. It's not always easy to know what to say to someone having a really rough time, so an inspirational quote or encouraging Scripture is great. Adding "I'm thinking of you today" or "praying for you" makes it personal, and a short "no need to respond" takes away any pressure to get back to you. To make it super easy for you, I have some you can download for free at www.nikihardy.com /breatheagaingifts.

Post a funny card. Snail mail is such a delight, and a funny card helps us laugh when all we want to do is scream. One day I opened a card that read, "Laughter is the best medicine. Unless you have diarrhea. Then I'd recommend Imodium." As you can imagine, it made my day. I like to keep a stash of cards at home so I can send them when I think of someone. And since American mail carriers collect from our doorstep, I don't even need to leave home.

Give a restaurant gift card. If you're out to dinner, add a gift card to your check so it's ready to give someone who needs either a date night or an easy dinner. It's a lovely treat to "have to" go out for dinner or get a free pass on cooking.

Take them a meal. I used to get my knickers in a twist about this, worrying that my Neanderthal cooking skills weren't up to the task. But since being on the receiving end of many meals, I've come to see the true gift is in not having to shop, prep, cook, or even think about what on earth to cook. Love in a casserole dish is always gratefully received no matter how simple the food. When I take someone a meal, I simply cook double of what we're having for dinner and put it in a disposable container so no one needs to worry about washing up or returning dishes. If I'm super busy I pick up a shop-bought meal with some fresh salad or fruit. Popping a card on top is a nice touch too.

Volunteer your children as sitters, dog walkers, and helpers. This one is a triple win. You get to love your friend, they get their dog walked, lawn mowed, or toddlers watched, and your kids get a lesson in loving others. Bingo!

Pray for them. I loved it when people asked me how they could pray for me—and then did! Any prayer is a good prayer, but asking someone what specific prayer requests they have shows them you care, you're interested, and you believe God listens and acts.

Make them a playlist. When I went in for my first surgery, a friend gave me her old iPod with nothing but worship music on it. It was such a gift—I played it in the quiet darkness of the hospital and it kept me sane and tethered to Jesus. If you want to share songs but don't want to hand over a complete iPod, I made a "Breathe Again" playlist for you to enjoy yourself and share with a friend. You can find it at www.niki hardy.com/breatheagaingifts.

Run errands. If your tough season is taking an emotional toll rather than a physical one, you may still be able to help others whose physical needs are more limited. We can pick up groceries or prescriptions, or run to the post office. It's easier when we tag these on to our own errands, and a simple text saying something like "I'm off to the supermarket this afternoon. Need anything while I'm out?" makes the person we're helping feel less of a burden.

Listen well. Asking how someone's doing *today* tells them you understand how up and down their journey can be and you care about how they are right this minute. Remembering their answer and checking back later lets them know you weren't just being polite when you asked. Given my memory is rather sieve-like, I sometimes make notes to remind myself. It's so important to allow someone to feel angry, negative, and worried without trying to solve everything. When we agree life stinks, expressing how sorry we are they are going through this, it's not just loving—it shows deep empathy and tells someone their pain is valid. The added benefit is it takes away any pressure we feel to have answers or fix it. When friends sat in the brokenness with me, agreed it was a nightmare, and didn't try to fix it, I felt so loved.

Hug and hold on. Not everyone is a hugger like me, but human touch can be the connection someone needs when they are already feeling alone and overwhelmed. Cancer isn't contagious, nor is miscarriage or depression, and if your friend's kid is on drugs, hugging her won't turn your teenagers into addicts.

To get over any awkwardness I simply smile, open my arms, and say, "I'm a hugger." Then I step toward them, hug, hold on for that extra squeeze before releasing them and smiling again as I step back. Easy! Or simply lay a hand on someone's shoulder as they tell you their story—it says, "I'm with you."

Share what worked for you. When you're unsure what to say, it's easy to fill the space with either your own story or how Great-Uncle Bob had that or how your next-door neighbor's cat's grandmother once knew a woman who went through the same thing. But please, for the love of all things sane, *don't*. If by any chance you've been through the same thing or something similar, sharing what worked for you (not what you think they should do—there's a big difference) is way more loving. It's both kind and helpful to say, "Oh gosh, that's so hard. When x happened to me, I found y really helped. Maybe you could try that."

Gandalf was right when he said, "It is the small everyday deeds of ordinary folk that keep the darkness at bay . . . small acts of kindness and love."[1] Kindness isn't costly and adds up over time as we chip away at the darkness. Then, as we love—little and often—what we receive far exceeds what we can ever give out.

Love doesn't always mean leaping into action; often it's simply stepping toward someone in love. Today may not be the day to start a worldwide ministry or take in your neighbor's ailing mother-in-law, but today will always be the day to hold out a hand and say, "Me too. I hate that you're going through this."

If you've focused on self-preservation in this difficult season, I get it. I was right there with you until Vicki and I met in our matching gowns. Please don't beat yourself up. Instead, let me invite you to lift your eyes from your own swirling life to look around and see what you already have to give someone nearby who could use a small act of kindness.

When we reach out in love at little cost to ourselves, we offer something priceless while receiving something invaluable. Let's see each other not as burdens with the potential to break us but as fellow travelers equally in need of love and encouragement. If we can do that, we not only chip away at each other's darkness but lighten the way ahead for us both.

I am a Thriver.

I believe life doesn't have to be pain-free to be full.

I reject the lies of the world about who and whose I am.

I embrace the truth that I am loved, seen, and enough, and that God loves me, isn't mad, and will never leave.

I've got this because God's got me, and together we can do more than I could ever do alone.

I choose brave, knowing it doesn't need to be big, just intentional.

I trust God, even when I don't want to and can't sense his presence, because I've checked his credentials and can let go of everything I've been clinging to.

I lean into community because thriving is a team sport and no one wins alone.

I step into vulnerable spaces with God and others, aware that my strength can be my biggest weakness.

I embrace the good, the bad, and the ugly of my journey, knowing the only way out is through and there's life and healing to be found along the way.

I practice gratitude in all things, confident that peace and well-being will follow.

I reach out in small acts of kindness, gaining far more than I could ever give.

LEARNING TO BREATHE AGAIN

How have you believed the myth of costly kindness? When has the idea of reaching out filled you with dread, preventing you from doing so?

Read Matthew 7:12; Luke 6:38; and 2 Corinthians 1:4. What do these verses say you'll receive as you give out in small ways?

Name three people in your life whose load you might lighten with a small act of kindness. How might you do that? Perhaps it's just a phone call, an encouraging card, or a text. (Check out my list of ideas in this chapter if you're stuck.) If your ideas lighten their load but overwhelm you, scrap them and try again!

As you reach out, name some of the ways you have been filled in return, making a note so you can practice gratitude for how God has met you in this way.

———■———

Lord, thank you for always being there for me, always stepping out and loving me even when I've lacked the capacity to love others. I'm so sorry I've shied away from reaching out. I've been frightened of adding their mess to mine and drowning.

Show me who to go to and how to love them well. I want to reach out to the people you put in front of me, blessing them as we travel this rocky road together. I can only give out of the love you pour into me, so fill me up, Lord—to the top, until it overflows.

In the name of your Son, Jesus, who reached out to all humanity in the greatest act of kindness the world has ever seen. Amen.

PART 3

Keep Calm and Breathe On

—11—

Now What?

Have tools, will travel

Yesterday is gone. Tomorrow has not yet come. We only have today. Let us begin.

Mother Teresa

And I am sure of this, that he who began a good work in you will bring it to completion at the day of Jesus Christ.

Philippians 1:6 ESV

When Jesus refers to us as sheep in John 10, I'm pretty sure it's not a compliment. I don't think he's calling us cute, fluffy, snuggable creatures, but implying we're rather needy, stupid animals with a tendency to wander off, who fall over and can't get up without help, and who are utterly lost without him. I have to say that description fits me to a T.

KEEP CALM AND BREATHE ON

I follow people and things that aren't my shepherd, I go wandering off, and I get knocked off my feet, lying with my legs in the air and bleating helplessly for days.

Even when life in my little sheep world is good and happy, I need his rod and staff to guide me out of the safety of my sheep pen into wide-open pastures where there's ample food and life to be had. How much more do we need our Shepherd when life is more tornados and tarantulas than rainbows and unicorns? Like sheep of little intelligence, we stay tucked in the safety of our sheep pens, unaware or unwilling to step out and discover what's waiting outside. There's a whole pasture with freedom to roam, breathe, frolic, and waggle our little sheep tails with glee. It's in these wide-open spaces we find freedom and joy and laughter; it's where we find the freshest grass, and where we get to be fully ourselves, fully alive, even if life doesn't look like a Martha Stewart commercial.

Out into Wide-Open Spaces

The context of John 10:1–9 is Jesus's invitation into wide-open pasture, and it's his continued and constant call and encouragement to us because he's always got more for us. He calls us out because he loves every one of his sheep—no matter how stupid or how far we wander off—and he hates to see us trampled and shipwrecked by life. He wants us to live fully alive, confident we are known, loved, and precious, seen, forgiven, and valued. Our Shepherd came so we may live abundantly, with abounding, overflowing life in him. He always has more for us, now and forever.

Now that you've been through all seven practices, I pray you've stepped out of your sheep pen and started to taste the fresh, succulent pasture of his life and breathe fresh air. That's exciting and I can't wait to hear about it. (Just email me, I promise to write back.)

But the Thief Will Come

I was locked in the loo, our flight was boarding, and I was kicking myself for having a green curry the night before. The thought of being strapped to a chair, unable to make a dash for the bathroom while being trapped in a small metal tube leaving the ground at speed only made things worse. I popped a couple of Imodium and prayed. These are my go-to remedies: prayer, Imodium, and Preparation H—the holy trinity of every rectal cancer survivor caught in an emergency.

My prayers were answered. I made it. No embarrassing explosions or mid-takeoff calls from the flight attendant for the woman in 24D to sit back down. Another bullet dodged.

I might be cancer-free, but rather annoyingly I'm not struggle-free. Life rarely is. Whether it's the inconvenience of a replumbed digestive system or worrying about Dad's PSA counts rising again, our challenge will always be to keep following Jesus out of the sheep pen day by day, often minute by minute. It's not easy. Storms whip through our lives, scattering debris far and wide, and as soon as one storm passes through, the horizon darkens with the next ominous onslaught.

Right before he promises his disciples "real and eternal life, more and better life than they ever dreamed of," Jesus warns that the enemy will come to steal, kill, and destroy (John 10:10). Boy, did he nail it. How often is a better life snatched from our grasp as we discover Mum's memory lapses are the beginnings of Alzheimer's, or the ex-boyfriend we still love deeply is getting married? When fear steals our joy, doubts kill any remnant of trust we were clinging to, or grief destroys our hope? Not to mention the next hard thing waiting to slap us around.

The bad news is the enemy is a devious @#$%&! and doesn't play fair.

The good news is the battle's already been won.

Thanks to the cross we don't fight *for* victory but *from* victory. Jesus's death and resurrection mean the battle's been won, once and for all, and we get to stand in victory with him. How great is that? Did you know you had that kind of power?

When Jesus made himself nothing, taking the nature of a servant and humbling himself by becoming obedient to death, even death on a cross (see Phil. 2:6–8), he gave us the gift not only of salvation, eternal life, and abundant life but of *victory* in him. We have authority over Satan, the thief. On the cross Jesus defeated the enemy, and now Satan is just trying to do as much damage as he can in his final death throes—damage to you and me and the abundant life we're living. So the bad news is there'll always be another storm cloud brewing and a thief to watch out for. But the good news is that even as troubles just keep coming, God has more abundant life to give us and won't stop calling us out into his pasture to receive it.

Our challenge will always be to keep on keeping on, to keep using the practices to live fully no matter what. They aren't just full-life-building practices; they are enemy-destroying practices. So, friend, I want to encourage you to take these tools and fight for your birthright—the right to thrive, not just survive.

Pack Your Tool Kit and Go

My ostomy bag (or as I liked to call it, my poop bag) and I were inseparable for six months. It was a miracle of modern medicine, freeing me to walk, talk, and poop all at the same time. But for all its medical brilliance and convenience, my little bag came with one big downside. As I've said before, it was temperamental and tended to leak. Now, I could handle this when I was at home, but heading off in public was daunting and stressful.

A wise soul advised me to make a little emergency pack to carry with me in case of leaks. I chose a cute little makeup pouch and filled it with everything I needed to change the bag and freshen up after an explosive emergency or leak. This little kit gave me the confidence to get out and about, knowing I was equipped to deal with whatever smelly crisis befell me. Oh the joys of rectal cancer. I still carry an emergency kit with me today, but the ostomy supplies have been replaced with Imodium, Preparation H, flushable wipes, lip balm, and headphones (how they always end up in there I'll never know).

Being told I had a tumor the size of a Double Stuf Oreo in my backside and my subsequent slow demise into pure survival mode were the catalysts to finding these seven practices and learning to squeeze the most out of life despite everything. Like my bathroom emergency kit, they now travel with me wherever I go.

They are one of the many ways I constantly try to follow my Shepherd out into the wider, more open spaces of my life where I know he will feed and fill me no matter what's going on.

I use these practices pretty much every week, if not every day. Whether my world is mildly shaken, moderately stirred, or massively shattered, I whip them out to see which one I need for the job at hand. If I'm struggling with a friend who hurt my feelings, I dive into my bag for *vulnerability* and *choosing brave*. When our teenagers aren't home and their curfew has come and gone, I dig deep to find *trusting God* and pray for the bonus of parenting wisdom. During my annual scans I lie there as the machine cranks around me and *practice gratitude* for God bringing me this far. When my uncle David died last year, leaving me with feelings more of longing and nostalgia than grief, I wondered what it would look like to *embrace the journey* through this tangle of sadness and yearning for my childhood instead of running away.

Using the practices rarely changes our external circumstances; instead, the shift is internal. We see things differently, noticing love and connection, paths through the maze, or an escaping smile or giggle that we previously held back. We begin to thrive where once we'd only survived. It's not perfect (not even close), but that's okay because now we begin to see God's rubies where once there was only rubble.

If life really is 10 percent what happens to us and 90 percent how we react to it,[1] and I believe it is, we have the power to influence at least 90 percent of how we experience life. That's huge and terribly exciting. So, whatever comes our way, let's react time and time again with these life-giving practices, and God will turn our less-than lives into the more-than lives he came to give us.

Use It or Lose It

It wasn't surprising my shot missed the goal. What was surprising was my playing high school lacrosse again in my midforties. It felt so good—if I ignored my burning lungs and the lead in my quads. It turns out you can take the girl out of the game but not the game out of the girl.

I fell in love with lacrosse in my first year of secondary school (the equivalent of sixth grade here in the USA) when I sported a chocolate-brown gym skirt, uneven pigtails, and an innocent desire to fit in at a school where Jo and Claire had already blazed a rebellious trail. As I sat with my old wooden stick on the red London bus I took home from school each afternoon, I did my best to ignore the local high schoolers' jokes about the butterfly net wedged at my feet.

Thirty years later I was back on the field as assistant varsity coach at our kids' school, and that day I'd jumped at the chance to make up the numbers when the girls scrimmaged at the end of practice. The trouble was, my heart was keen, my flesh was willing, and I'd even studied the updated rules, but my skills were rusty—horribly rusty. Hence the missed shot. Did I mention it missed by a looooooong way?

Use it or lose it. That's what experts say about fitness, speaking another language, and your local bookstore, and I can tell you it's definitely true for lacrosse skills. As I thundered toward the goal, the defenders crashing in for a double-team just as we'd practiced, I knew what I needed to do: dodge, fake, and aim at the corners. Except I'd lost the reflex to do it without thinking, so it felt wooden and forced and I missed by a mile.

I'd hate for you to close the final chapter of this book and have the same be true for you. After all, you've made it this far, read all the way here, learned new mind-sets, made the practices your own, and worked through some pretty tough stuff. You can't let that hard work go to waste. These practices are for every—yes, *every*—day, not just the really tough ones. If we leave them in the back of the closet along with our thin jeans and the boots we bought on sale because we loved the price tag more than the design, they'll gather dust, forgotten. Then, when life's crashing in on us, sticks raised and screaming loudly, we'll forget how to use them. We'll miss the goal and life will win.

So let's pop these practices in our bags and set off into the world, equipped for anything. Whatever life sends crashing your way, big or small, you'll be equipped to score.

Remember How Far You've Come

You know what I should have done? I should have asked you to take a snapshot of your life before you started this book so you could take another one today and compare the two.

I love pictures of me the year after my son James was born. I look like a pea. I'm completely round—my face so saucer-like it resembled a full moon when I smiled—and I remember what a baby I was in my faith, having only met Jesus a couple of years before. But that's not why I love them. It's not just the smile that creeps across my face as I see my now twenty-one-year-old son nestled in my arms, but I look at myself now and see how far I've come. How my faith has grown like Jack's beanstalk and the fifty pounds have come and gone (well, almost). And like any good before and after comparison, it stirs up hope, encouragement, and most of all, motivation.

So let me ask you, what did life look like before you dived into this book? How did you feel when you cracked open the first pages? Tired, exhausted, and overwhelmed? Wondering how much more you could take and when this heartache would end? Skeptical there was more? Willing to try anything because, quite frankly, it couldn't get much worse?

Now how do you feel? I'm not asking you to look at your circumstances and see if things have changed for the better (but that would be brilliant for sure). Rather, consider how connected you are to God and others and whether you look at life differently. Has what you believe to be true about yourself, God, and what this life can hold changed, even if diddly-squat has changed around you? Do you believe God has more for you? Have you started to taste life's sweetness on the tip of your tongue amongst the bitter and sour of what you've been dealing with? Most of all, are you breathing again?

Take a moment to think about then and now. If you had an abundance-ometer, would it have risen? How are your joy, peace, comfort, and trust levels? Have your laughter, gratitude, and hope tanks filled up since you began? If they have, celebrate! Tell someone. Email me—I'd love to celebrate with you. Share it with the world or your dog. Mark your progress. Small wins matter and slowly build; every little bit counts.

I pray you dug up a ruby buried in the rubble of a relationship, a diagnosis, or another hard situation. That would be wonderful. Hold it up to the light, marvel at its beauty, and let it shine. Enjoy the gift it is. If you've found one, you can uncover more. If you've taken one relaxing, life-giving breath, you can take another.

Even if your current battle has no end in sight, or if you can see the next one heading down the tracks as this one leaves the station, please know you are loved, seen, precious, and not forgotten—by me or by God. You've got this because he's got you. What a team you make. He loves you, is with you, will not leave you, and has abundant life for you now and always.

Remember, life doesn't have to be pain-free to be full. Now go live it.

I am a Thriver, not just a survivor.

I know how to find more whenever life hands me less.

I have learned to breathe again.

The Thriver's Manifesto

I am a Thriver.

I believe life doesn't have to be pain-free to be full.

I reject the lies of the world about who and whose I am.

I embrace the truth that I am loved, seen, and enough, and that God loves me, isn't mad, and will never leave.

I've got this because God's got me, and together we can do more than I could ever do alone.

I choose brave, knowing it doesn't need to be big, just intentional.

I trust God, even when I don't want to and can't sense his presence, because I've checked his credentials and can let go of everything I've been clinging to.

I lean into community because thriving is a team sport and no one wins alone.

I step into vulnerable spaces with God and others, aware that my strength can be my biggest weakness.

I embrace the good, the bad, and the ugly of my journey, knowing the only way out is through and there's life and healing to be found along the way.

I practice gratitude in all things, confident that peace and well-being will follow.

I reach out in small acts of kindness, gaining far more than I could ever give.

I am a Thriver, not just a survivor.

I know how to find more whenever life hands me less.

I have learned to breathe again.

(To download a printable version of this manifesto, hop over to www.nikihardy.com/breatheagaingifts.)

Gifts

From me to you, with love

- The Thriver's Manifesto (printable)

- "Life doesn't have to be pain-free to be full" (printable)

- "5 Steps to Trusting God When You Don't Feel Like It" (infographic)

- "Breathe Again" playlist

- Scripture images to text to a friend

- A Love Letter from God (printable and audio versions)

All these resources are my gift to you and are available to download at www.nikihardy.com/breatheagaingifts.

Resources

Where can I find help with . . . ?

Trust-Building Biographies

Laura Hillenbrand, *Unbroken*

Jackie Pullinger, *Chasing the Dragon: One Woman's Struggle against the Darkness of Hong Kong's Drug Den*

Joni Eareckson Tada, *Joni: An Unforgettable Story*

Corrie ten Boom, *The Hiding Place*

Nick Vujicic, *Life Without Limits*

Brother Yun, *The Heavenly Man*

Books for Hard Seasons

Kate Bowler, *Everything Happens for a Reason: And Other Lies I've Loved*

Brené Brown, *Rising Strong*

Melanie Dale, *It's Not Fair: Learning to Love the Life You Didn't Choose*

Bethany Hamilton, *Soul Surfer: A True Story of Faith, Family, and Fighting to Get Back on the Board*

Timothy Keller, *Walking with God through Pain and Suffering*

Sue Monk Kidd, *When the Heart Waits: Spiritual Direction for Life's Sacred Questions*

C. S. Lewis, *The Problem of Pain*

Shauna Niequist, *Bittersweet: Thoughts on Change, Grace, and Learning the Hard Way*

Bekah Jane Pogue, *Choosing Real: An Invitation to Celebrate When Life Doesn't Go as Planned*

Sheryl Sandberg and Adam Grant, *Option B: Facing Adversity, Building Resilience and Finding Joy*

Kristen Strong, *Girl Meets Change: Truths to Carry You through Life's Transitions*

Barbara Brown Taylor, *Learning to Walk in the Dark*

Philip Yancey, *Disappointment with God: Questions No One Asks Aloud*

Philip Yancey, *Where Is God When It Hurts?*

Acknowledgments

*Because I can't fit a hundred
names on the cover*

Twelve years ago I sat quietly as an older, wiser couple prayed for me and listened to the Lord on my behalf. They felt God might be saying something about writing, but I laughed. I hadn't written anything more than a thank-you note, science paper, or email since I was sixteen. Six years later and sick with cancer, I listened as another older, wiser woman prayed for me. We'd never met and she had no idea I was battling cancer, but the first words out of her mouth were, "You will not die, but you will preach the word of the Lord." My eyes snapped open in shock. But still I hadn't written a word.

All that to say, my first thanks must, as always, go to my God. You saw me, never left me, and set me free to do what I now love—encourage others to step further up and further in to you, the One who's always loved them. I love you.

To Al, the best cheerleader, tea maker, panic calmer, and putter-of-shape-and-form-to-my-first-crappy-draft-er. Your name should be on the cover right alongside mine. I love you. Thank you for believing in me before I did. You're the man. You're *my* man.

James, Sophie, and Emma, you are stronger, better people because cancer came into our lives, and yet I wish you'd never had to endure that journey. You've waited patiently outside hundreds of bathrooms only to wait for me to finish this book. I'm back! Anyone for Rummikub and nachos?

Mum and Jo, you've inspired me every step of the way. If I can encourage one person to live with as much dignity, humor, and strength as you, I'll be thrilled.

Claire, the distance between us may be counted in miles, but in my mind you live right next door. You dropped everything and came right at the start when our hearts were still broken. Thank you for inspiring me and reminding me that with Jesus all things are possible. I love you.

Dad and Cally, you've lived this painful, upside-down journey with openness, honesty, and love. Thank you for coming when I needed you.

Winn, Jennifer, Jill, Noelle, Lindsay, and Barb: Thank you. I have no words. You carried the load when I couldn't.

CityChurch, thank you for being the true body of Christ and the hands and feet of Jesus. Thank you for loving me.

Myquillyn Smith, for some strange reason you believed in me, offering me grace, truth, and an endorsement before I'd written a word. Thank you, friend.

To all my hope*writers friends, and cofounders Emily P. Freeman, Gary Morland, and Brian Dixon: I wouldn't be here without you. I just wouldn't. You mean so much to me, and there isn't room to name the many ways you've helped me, cheered me on, shown me the way, and talked me off the quitting ledge. Thank you.

"God does nothing except in response to believing prayer" (John Wesley), especially the prayers of the best Prayer Squad ever. Thank you.

Tamara Burdon, you jumped at the chance to brainstorm a few often-forgotten women of the Bible. Your love of the Word is contagious—keep writing.

Kathy Izard, thank you for coffee, crepes, wisdom, and the gift of writing in the mountains.

To my BASU friends (you know who you are), thank you for loving me well, sending ridiculous GIFs, sharing my words, and being the best "grace ninjas."

Amanda Luedeke, you took a chance on me and I'm forever grateful. You've held my hand and walked me through this journey with wisdom and a sense of humor. Thank you.

Renee Fisher, what can I say? Thank you for connecting me with Amanda and cheering me on.

Kelsey and the Revell team (Eileen Hanson, Patti Brinks, Amy Nemecek, and others), you saw something in me and my writing I didn't know was there. Thank you for helping it shine.

Helen Van Wagenen, my very first freditor. Thank you for reading my words when the most I could dream was that they'd make a great giveaway!

My Creative Help Voxer group, you're just the bee's knees. I love you.

Bekah Pogue, God didn't make a mistake when he connected us. I wish we lived next door and could sit together as the sun goes down, sipping wine on our porch. How is your heart today?

Tracy Steel, I love you, my fierce friend (despite your love of bows and polka dots!).

Colontown, the home of the original Thrivers. Thank you for loving this community-phobic Brit and inspiring me beyond belief.

To all my Thrivers: Becky, Todd, Joy, Kristan, Grace, Erin, and Ali. Thank you for sharing your stories so vulnerably and for shining God's light in the darkest places.

Notes

Who said what, where

I'm Sorry You're Here . . . No Wait, I Take That Back

1. Sheryl Sandberg and Adam Grant, *Option B: Facing Adversity, Building Resilience, and Finding Joy* (New York: Knopf, 2017), 10.

Chapter 1 Rubbish We Believe When the Poop Hits the Fan

1. Maria Furlough, *Breaking the Fear Cycle: How to Find Peace for Your Anxious Heart* (Grand Rapids: Revell, 2018), 17.

2. Martin E. P. Seligman, *Learned Optimism: How to Change Your Mind and Your Life* (New York: Pocket Books, 1991), quoted in Sandberg and Grant, *Option B*, 16.

Chapter 2 The Truth We Need When Our World Is Rocked

1. Ann Voskamp, *The Way of Abundance: A 60-Day Journey into a Deeply Meaningful Life* (Grand Rapids: Zondervan, 2018), 80.

2. Rick Warren, "Your Ministry of Reconciliation," Daily Hope with Rick Warren, November 8, 2015, https://www.crosswalk.com/devotionals/daily-hope-with-rick-warren/your-ministry-of-reconciliation-daily-hope-with-rick-warren-nov-8-2015.html.

3. Timothy Keller, *Walking with God through Pain and Suffering* (New York: Penguin, 2013), 58.

4. I heard Robert Madu say this in a talk at the Holy Trinity Brompton Leadership Conference, May 4, 2015.

Chapter 3 Practice Makes Better, Not Perfect

1. From Leta Wither's memorial order of service, July 12, 2016. Reproduced with permission.

Chapter 4 Choose Brave

1. Becky L. McCoy, "My Story," *Becky L. McCoy* (blog), https://beckyl mccoy.com/about/.

2. https://www.goodreads.com/quotes/1270897-courage-doesn-t -mean-you-don-t-get-afraid-courage-means-you

3. Lysa TerKeurst, "Choosing Grace," First 5 Bible Reading App, http://first5.org/plans/1-2%20Samuel/ff_samuel_25/.

4. Private email correspondence with the author, August 6, 2016.

Chapter 5 Trust God

1. https://www.brainyquote.com/quotes/mike_tyson_382439.

2. https://www.brainyquote.com/quotes/marshall_mcluhan_130541.

3. George MacDonald, *Phantastes* (London: Smith, Elder & Co., 1858), 323.

4. Private email correspondence with the author, July 19, 2017.

5. Phone call with the author in Fall 2016.

6. Erin Brown Hollis, *Cheers to the Diaper Years: 10 Truths for Thriving While Barely Surviving* (Savage, MN: Broadstreet, 2018), 61.

Chapter 6 Find Community

1. For more on this idea, see Tracy Wilde, *Finding the Lost Art of Empathy: Connecting Human to Human in this Disconnected World* (New York: Howard Books, 2017).

2. Eric Dregni, "Why Is Norway the Happiest Place on Earth?," *Star Tribune*, June 11, 2017, http://www.startribune.com/the-height-of-happy /427321393/#1.

3. Susan Pinker, "The Secret to Living Longer May Be Your Social Life," TED Talk, April 2017, https://www.ted.com/talks/susan_pinker _the_secret_to_living_longer_may_be_your_social_life.

4. L. J. Ferris, J. Jetten, P. Molenberghs, B. Bastian, F. Karnadewi, "Increased Pain Communication following Multiple Group Memberships Salience Leads to a Relative Reduction in Pain-Related Brain Activity," *PLoS ONE*, September 22, 2016, http://journals.plos.org/plosone/article?id=10.1371/journal.pone.0163117.

5. Sandberg and Grant, *Option B*, 128.

6. Kristen Strong, *Girl Meets Change: Truths to Carry You through Life's Transitions* (Grand Rapids: Revell, 2015), 153.

7. See Matt. 27:56; Mark 15:40; Luke 8:2–3.

8. Brené Brown, "The Power of Vulnerability," TED Talk, January 3, 2011, https://www.youtube.com/watch?v=iCvmsMzlF7o&t=259s.

Chapter 7 Be Vulnerable

1. Brené Brown, *Daring Greatly: How the Courage to Be Vulnerable Transforms the Way We Live, Love, Parent, and Lead* (New York: Avery Press, 2017), 37.

2. Ferris et al., "Increased Pain Communication."

3. Brené Brown, *The Gifts of Imperfection: Let Go of Who You Think You're Supposed to Be and Embrace Who You Are* (Center City, MI: Hazelden Publishing, 2010), 49.

Chapter 8 Embrace the Journey

1. Michael Rosen and Helen Oxenbury, *We're Going on a Bear Hunt* (New York: Little Simon, 1997).

2. Susan David, "The Gift and Power of Emotional Courage," TEDWomen 2017, https://www.ted.com/talks/susan_david_the_gift_and_power_of_emotional_courage/transcript?language=en.

3. David, "The Gift and Power of Emotional Courage," 15:28.

4. See Isa. 41:10; Deut. 31:6; Matt. 28:20.

5. A reference to chapters 15 and 16 of C. S. Lewis, *The Last Battle* (New York: HarperCollins, 1956).

Chapter 9 Practice Gratitude

1. Amy Morin, "7 Scientifically Proven Benefits of Gratitude That Will Motivate You to Give Thanks Year-Round," *Forbes*, November 23, 2014, https://www.forbes.com/sites/amymorin/2014/11/23/7-scientifically-proven-benefits-of-gratitude-that-will-motivate-you-to-give-thanks-year-round/&refURL=&referrer=.

2. Corrie ten Boom, *The Hiding Place*, 35th anniversary edition (Grand Rapids: Chosen, 2006), 210.

3. Corrie ten Boom, *The Hiding Place*, 220.

4. Bekah Pogue, *Choosing Real: An Invitation to Celebrate When Life Doesn't Go as Planned* (Uhrichville, OH: Shiloh Run Press, 2016), 143.

5. Morin, "7 Scientifically Proven Benefits of Gratitude."

6. Robert Emmons, "How Gratitude Can Help You Through Hard Times," *Greater Good Magazine*, May 13, 2013, https://greatergood.berkeley.edu/article/item/how_gratitude_can_help_you_through_hard_times.

Chapter 10 Reach Out

1. From the scene "Galadriel," in *The Hobbit: An Unexpected Journey*, directed by Peter Jackson (MGM, 2012), DVD, 1:40:29.

Chapter 11 Now What?

1. Charles R. Swindoll quotes, https://www.goodreads.com/author/quotes/5139.Charles_R_Swindoll.

About the Author

Niki's sensible(ish) bio

Niki is a Brit in the USA, rectal (yes, rectal) cancer Thriver, pastor's wife, tea drinker, and teller of bad jokes. Her speaking and writing offer encouragement, truth, practical resources, and a humorous dollop of reality so you can thrive, no matter what life throws at you. If she can't hug you in person, she'd love to connect with you and hopefully hear your story at www.nikihardy.com.

Educated in Oxford, England, she now lives in Charlotte, NC, with her family. Her work has appeared in *Christian Today*, *RELEVANT*, Woman to Woman (Premier Radio), ThriveMom, and Living By Design Ministries. When she's not speaking, writing, or running trails with her Doodles, you can find her with a nice cup of tea, trying to figure out which remote control actually turns the TV on.

Connect with Niki

Find more of Niki's resources and her speaking schedule at WWW.NIKIHARDY.COM

● ● ● ●

Connect with Niki online (if she can't hug you in person)

f NikiHardyauthor   **🐦** NikiBHardy   **📷** niki.hardy